Reclaim Your Power

A journey through archetypes
to remember, reclaim, and
rebirth your true feminine
power and wholeness.

Praise

"Through the *Reclaim Your Power Pathway*, Laura Swan brilliantly illuminates the passageway into the deep Feminine that resides in our individual and collective psyche. With grace and compassion, she gently guides women in awakening to their inner feminine archetypes and in discovering the immense power of sisterhood. I highly recommend this journey to any woman seeking to re-member and re-claim the essence, power, and wisdom of her Feminine nature."

~ Anita Johnston, Ph.D, Author, *Eating in the Light of the Moon*
& the Light of the Moon Café

"Laura has woven together a remarkable resource for women at exactly the right moment in history. The world urgently needs for humanity to come back into balance, and women are being called to offer their deepest wisdom and authentic feminine power NOW. By giving us glimpses of her own journey through trauma and pain and self-doubt and healing and love and joy, Laura invites us all to show up as we are – and then challenges us to take the next step and the next in our own leadership. I see all around me how important it is for women to accept the leadership challenges of this moment, and I also see how difficult many of us find it to really step into our full expression. Women struggle with profound archetypal and generational issues related to self-worth as a natural reaction to thousands of years of the domination and subjugation of all things feminine. I applaud this brave book written by this wise young woman to remind us it is time to embrace the many dimensions of our own wisdom and power."

~ **Kathe Schaaf**, Co-Founder of Gather the Women and Women of Spirit and Faith, Co Editor of Women, Spirituality and Transformative Leadership: Where Grace Meets Power

"I absolutely love the work Laura is doing in the world with women... I hope all women join her programs and follow her because we need so much more of what she is offering out there in the world. Thank you for being a true visionary leader, Laura, and empowering women to lead from love!"

~ **Lynne Twist**, Global Visionary Leader, Humanitarian, Author of the *Soul of Money*, and Founder of the Soul of Money Institute and the Pachamama Foundation

"Laura J. Swan has created the one and only guidebook that you'll ever need to remember, reclaim, and rebirth yourself as a Divine Woman. She will help you activate the Archetypes within that need to be called forth, and help you to access your power whenever you need to... over and over again. Laura, your work is a true gift and blessing, thank you!"

~ **Chong Lee**, Women's Lifestyle Business Mentor & Clean Energy Tech Entrepreneur

"*Reclaim Your Power* has helped me to love myself, accept myself and understand myself so much more than ever before. Laura has a beautiful way of guiding us through this journey of listening to our own inner voice and healing from within. Her love and passion are so clearly illustrated through this work. Knowing that she has also healed herself with this process and shares from her own knowledge and experience has given me the hope that I need to take each step."

~ **Rebecca Rae**, Women's Empowerment Leader

"If you are looking for a leader who walks her talk and embodies her message, look no further than Laura J. Swan. She is the real deal."

~ **Debbie Lichter,** Congruency Mentor and Food Addiction Expert

"Delicate in nature yet fierce with love. She weaves this way of being in her coaching, sistership circles, and teachings to give every woman permission to tap into this feminine power of harmony, creative expression and impact. Working with Laura Swan will give you the courage to step into owning your voice and creating a life with purpose and love."

~ **Novalena J. Nichele,** Author of the *Total Female Package*

"Laura's writings and teachings propel people to greatness. I have had the absolute privilege and honor to have been personally mentored by Laura and every single aspect of my life has moved forward in the very best possible direction. I know that absolutely everyone can benefit from the wisdom, love, and grace in her book, *Reclaim Your Power.* She is a magical and beautiful light in this world."

~ **Dawn Witte,** Author of *"Be..."*, CEO of I Give On, and Founder of
The Desire to Inspire Foundation

"Laura J. Swan's impeccable work has delivered a profound and beautiful impact to my life. As a healer and woman discovering my own greatness, claiming my divine power and stepping into my Dharmic path as a leader, I'm absolutely honored to call Laura a mentor and friend. Laura's masterful intuition and clairvoyance has been a brilliant reflection of my truth, building my confidence in ways which are nurturing my soul in preparation to fully embody the brilliance that I've always known to be my true potential."

~ **Ali Mae Thompson,** Light Worker, Healing Artist, Kundalini Yoga Instructor

"Working with Laura has saved my life. Her coaching, circles, and retreats have helped me break through life-long addictions, and have prepared me for the journey of stepping into my divine feminine... mentally, physically and spiritually here on this planet. I will forever be in gratitude for my sister Laura for creating a space for my essence to blossom... and to feel truly supported, honored and loved."

   ~ **Ashley Diaz**, Buti Yoga Teacher, Addiction and Recovery Coach

"Laura is an amazing leader. She is aware and loving; a woman I trust and am so proud to call my sister! Because I said YES to Laura's programs, I am a much stronger woman with a big presence to bring more love and light into the world for our children and the next 7 generations to come!"

   ~ **Michelle Little**, Humanitarian, Activist, Founder of Beautiful Dying

"Laura creates an incredible space of love and safety that provides women with both transformative experiences and a beautiful sense of community. Her ability to accept and honor people exactly where they are on their journey is a unique gift. At the same time, she is a strong and courageous presence that inspires others to step into their full power as well."

~ **Rachel Parks**, Corporate Executive Success Coach

"Laura Swan is a woman who embodies the essence of love in her life and leadership. As a co-facilitator and leader, I feel blessed to have worked with her and next to her. She is a woman who is truly sharing her gifts, and making a huge impact in this world with her heart."

~ **Jess Magic**, Speaker, HeARTist, Sacred Activist

"Laura has always had a gift for bringing women together and making each individual feel showered with love. I feel so blessed to know her. Sitting in the flow of her grace is one of my favorite places to be!"

~ **Karen Kripalani,** Author, Mother, Photographer, Co-founder of
OceanHouse Media

"I found Laura to be inspirational and a beautiful role model of an embodied woman with a big heart. She has created a very professional and comprehensive program, created from love and always held lovingly by Laura. It was a nourishing experience with many insights and wisdom gained intellectually and emotionally. Thank you, Laura!"

~ **Caroline Roberts,** Massage Therapist and Baby Massage Instructor

"Laura taught me how to love and honor myself. With Laura's leadership, I learned how to safely release my insecurities, untruths, self-doubts and uncertainties. In addition to monthly circles, I went on three weekend retreats where we would celebrate our victories, practice yoga, sit in sacred space, dance and celebrate our inner Goddess. I will never forget those special and sacred times, and often thank the universe for Laura's commitment to helping me heal myself and for bringing us together. Whatever understanding of the power of universal love I have, I owe it to Laura. I will forever live to love, serve and remember."

~ **Maureen M**, Holistic Nutritionist, Belly Dancer, Yogini

Cover Design by Carolyn Sheltraw

Disclaimer: While journaling prompts are excellent tools for helping to relieve stress and encourage creativity and life balance, they are not substitutes for medical advice or professional counseling and support for depression or other conditions you might be experiencing. Please seek assistance if you need it.

Be well ... Laura

ISBN: 978-0-9993495-0-2

Reclaim Your Power

A journey through archetypes to remember, reclaim, and rebirth your true feminine power and wholeness.

Laura J. Swan

Dedication

To my children… my daughter Luna and my son Maui… this book is for you, and was inspired by my desire to make your world a better place for you and the many generations to come.

To my husband and fierce Warrior, Jonathan. I love you deeply. Thank you for seeing the Warrioress in me, and helping to call her forth so I can birth my dreams and Soul work in the world. I could not have done this without your love and support.

To my whole family who supported me to birth my visions and work over the years… I love you, and I thank you with all my heart for your love and patience, and for always believing in me in all my endeavors.

To all of my mentors, sisters and friends in my life today who have supported and empowered me to be the woman I want to be, and who have stood by me through thick and thin… I thank you with all my heart. I would not be here without you.

To my fiercely devoted editor and dear friend, Deborah, who stood by me through this process and made magic happen. You are a true Warrioress and I'm so very thankful for your support in helping me birth this baby (just in time before the real baby!).

To all the Wise Women, Ancestors, and Feminine Leaders who have come before me... thank you for paving the way. I bow to you, draw strength from you, and honor you every day.

To all the women over the years who have been a part of my circles, or have been my clients, or attended any of my events and programs... you are the ones who inspire me to do what I do, every day. I am eternally grateful to be of service to you, and to rise together in our missions to help heal the world.

And to God, the Goddess, the Great Mystery, and the Divine Feminine Spirit of Love and heart rising on this planet... I am in this life to be of service for you. Use me.

Xo
Laura

Contents

Introduction

Welcome, Sister… to the *Reclaim Your Power* pathway.

This book is meant to be an interactive, creative experience that will take you through different phases of evolution as a woman. It is a pathway of remembering, reclaiming, and rebirthing your true feminine power and wholeness, and an activation that invites you into your greatest creative potential in this life. We move through seven different energy centers and nine different feminine archetypes. Throughout our journey we integrate archetypal psychology, feminine spirituality, art therapy, energy medicine, mythology, music and mindset training for a holistic and multi-faceted approach.

For more of a creative and practical application of the material here, you can also choose to use the *Reclaim Your Power Companion*

Guidebook and Creativity Journal in addition to this book. The Companion Guidebook has journaling questions, coloring pages and guided exercises that will give you rich, well-rounded access to this material and expand upon all that we are exploring here. It also includes links to my website for free videos and audios where I guide you through interactive practices, meditations and visualizations.

All these written materials also can accompany the *Reclaim Your Power* program for women that I offer online. You are welcome to explore the program should you feel called to take this work even deeper. That program is offered virtually several times a year, and also has a self-study option for you to explore it at your own pace. Though the *Reclaim Your Power* 10-week online program we offer is a rich and potent experience that expands upon all that we cover here, this book stands alone as a powerful guided journey in and of itself.

The *Reclaim Your Power* pathway was born out of my seventeen-plus years of working with women in many different capacities. It has also come out of my personal journey of healing and reclaiming my own feminine power and wholeness so that I could create a life aligned with my truth and find authentic peace and happiness in my heart.

As a trained therapist, a certified women's life coach, a yoga teacher and an energy medicine teacher and practitioner, I have used many different modalities and tools in working with women. I have created here a pathway that integrates some of the best teachings and practices I know to help women heal and transform their lives, reclaim their power and step into the true calling they feel deep within their hearts. I have included my personal journey of how I came to know each of these practices in my own life.

This is a pathway of self-awareness and self-discovery that, ultimately, I pray will lead you back home to yourself… right back to your own powerful, creative and beautiful Soul. And I know this journey well, because it is the very path I have chosen to take for myself as a woman.

In my own life, I have had my share of challenges and trauma, from growing up in a broken family as a young girl, to drug and alcohol addiction by age eleven, to an abusive relationship at age thirteen, to a cancer scare at age fourteen, to shame around my body and sexuality in my teens, to a severe eating disorder in my early twenties. I struggled with many health challenges and fertility issues throughout the years and had numerous pregnancy losses before having my children. As I will share in some of my personal stories here, I have known the darkest of darkness and been in the deepest of depressions. I know what it feels like to want to give up on life altogether. Because at times… *it just felt too hard to go on.*

But by the grace of God, I did go on, and I have found a faith within me that has become unshakable and real. I came to discover, through these incredible challenges and times of darkness, the resilience of my Soul and the power of my own light. I believe I have created the life I live now, and stepped into my true calling, as a result of the lessons and hardships I endured. I believe with all my heart they have made me the woman I am today. And these lessons have all become part of this pathway that I share here with you.

> *There is a brokenness*
> *out of which comes the unbroken,*
> *a shatteredness*
> *out of which blooms the unshatterable.*
> *There is a sorrow*
> *beyond all grief which leads to joy*
> *and a fragility*
> *out of whose depths emerges strength.*
> *There is a hollow space*
> *too vast for words*
> *through which we pass with each loss,*
> *out of whose darkness*
> *we are sanctioned into being.*
> *There is a cry deeper than all sound*
> *whose serrated edges cut the heart*
> *as we break open to the place inside*
> *which is unbreakable and whole,*
> *while learning to sing.*

> ~ Rashani

I believe experiencing darkness and tragedy can become the fertile grounds for our greatest strength and gifts to be birthed. My experience has been that the most amazing women I know who are coaches, incredible mothers, healers, teachers, writers, entrepreneurs and more – most all of them have deeply known suffering and pain and have made what some would call "bad mistakes" and learned hard lessons along the way. This has been what made them, and has made us all, who we are today. And these are the women who are going to change the world (and already are right now).

One thing I have to say here before I go any further is that I truly love both women and men equally. I am a modern feminist, for sure... and I absolutely adore men and cherish their gifts. I am married to a driven, intensely passionate and very masculine man who has brought a critical and beautiful balance to my soft feminine nature and helped put me in touch with my own healthy masculine energy inside me.

I love masculine energy, and men. I believe that so much of the negativity and criticism that gets projected onto men as a group is not referring to the healthy masculine energy; it is referring to the wounded and out of balance masculine energy that has been running amuck on this planet for far too long (in both women and men). Our men need healing and balance just as much as our women do, and I want to proclaim that right here and now with all my heart.

With that said, I also believe that women are truly the most powerful, resilient and multi-dimensional creatures in the world. We are ridiculously strong and have unique flavors of compassion, empathy, vulnerability and nurturance coupled with fierceness, strength and power. We carry life and give birth, and we sacrifice our bodies over and over so that life can continue on this earth. We are a miracle (as are all creatures) and I do believe there is a very special power and strength that comes from being the bearers of life for a species. We HAVE to possess a certain type of emotional make-up to be able to do that without completely losing our shit and running for the hills (though I have to admit I almost have myself a few times).

The drive to nurture life within us and all around us, whether we birth actual children or not, is the same drive that also makes us great leaders, healers, feminine entrepreneurs and teachers, as well. We care deeply about other people's success, health, well-being and overall quality of life. We care deeply about building relationships and making sure they are maintained and healthy. We care deeply that not just some people, but all people, have the rights to a just and sustainable world.

And this is why we are being called to rise and reclaim the fullness of our gifts, our leadership and our creative potential like never before in human history. Because *we are needed now more than ever*. There are many challenges we face in this time that are pressing and urgent.

I believe that women's heart-centered leadership and wisdom is essential to our species' survival. Not only will owning our genuine gifts in service to the world make us happiest and most fulfilled (bonus), but also... our planet needs our love, creativity and vision right now like never before. We need as many of us as possible to be in our authentic power... because as women, our authentic power may be fierce, but it comes from our hearts and a genuine place of love.

> *"The world will be saved by the Western woman."*
> ~ The Dalai Lama

My deepest intention of this book and the *Reclaim Your Power* pathway is to support you in reclaiming the fullness of your true creative feminine power, and to help you discover how you can most effectively use it to heal yourself, create genuine happiness in your life, and help heal the world (should you feel called to do so). I hope with all my heart that you wake up to how remarkable you are and know how precious and important your gifts are at this time in human history, no matter who you are and what you have been through. Likely, the more difficult your story, the greater your "compassion training" has been, as I like to call it, and the more you have to give back to others as a result.

The qualities of genuine compassion and empathy are what make the most sensitive, dialed in leaders, teachers, mothers and healers in this world. We all have a story that has made us who we are today, and that has the power to give us more compassion. My hope is that through this reclaiming pathway, you reclaim all of your story and allow it to be alchemized into something beautiful for yourself the world. Because I know that women – the real and raw ones, the ones who feel deeply and intensely, and who may also have messy lives and wounded pasts –

hold the key to the transformation of our world. We are the resilient ones who know what it means to have suffered, and we also know what it means to emerge on the other side.

And right now… our world is fighting to emerge on the other side.

And we can do it. I know with all my heart we can. But we have to unite our hearts, empower each other and rise together. Women coming together in sisterhood and collaboration is one of the most important keys to our effectively using our feminine power to heal the world. We can no longer buy into the false, disempowering belief system that says other women are our competition – that if one woman has the man, the career, the body, the house – that it means other women must have less of their own dreams, or are any less worthy of obtaining them.

This myth of scarcity is all a lie and perpetuated by a culture around us that is constantly telling us we are not good enough. We are sold every gadget, supplement and diet out there because the essential hidden message within their marketing, and in all of our media and advertising, is that: "you're not good enough, pretty enough, smart enough, or thin enough as you are… so you need THIS MIRACLE PRODUCT to make you BETTER."

And we buy into it, time and time again.

This, and other deeply ingrained factors, perpetuates the false belief that because we are not enough, we have to compete with other women who we think may be inherently better than us (and so the cycle continues). But the truth is... *when one woman wins, we all win. When we empower each other with love and confidence, together we rise.* And my prayer is that we come together in this awakening and reclaiming process... and together we rise.

The three-part intention of this guidebook and the *Reclaim Your Power* pathway is to support you (and all women) to:

Remember, Reclaim and Rebirth... all of who you are.

It is my mission to help women shift out of an old paradigm of disempowerment, shame and self-criticism and come together to REMEMBER who we truly are inside... to RECLAIM our deepest feminine POWER... and to REBIRTH our authentic selves from our wholeness and full potential. From here we can truly change the world, and we are already today.

> *"We must be willing to let go of the life we planned so as to have the life that is waiting for us."*
> ~ Joseph Campbell

The Reclaim Your Power pathway is a fun and creative journey, one that will help you reclaim the youthful and joyful parts of yourself, as well as the sensual, passionate woman within you. I will take you deep into my own vulnerable process to give you some personal experiences of how this work can be applied. I hope to help you tap into your own wise, intuitive gifts, and allow you to explore different parts within you that are longing to be remembered, reclaimed, or discovered for the first time, just like they once were within me (and still are!). It is a pathway to integrate all parts of yourself so you can experience your wholeness and live a life authentic to your dreams and desires.

It is also a spiraling, circular journey that is constantly inviting you to evolve and transform. It invites you at times to ask difficult questions and peer into the darkness, as well as dive into colorful and fun explorations and exercises. I believe that in doing both... you can emerge even more connected to your own authentic light.

This is why I use the symbol of the spiral in so much of my work and art. To me, it has become representative of the constant evolution of our feminine journey, as well as a symbol of the infinite power of creativity and fertility within the woman's body and Soul.

Sometimes, when we are moving back to the center of the spiral, we are going deep within ourselves, perhaps into a dark or challenging time, or sometimes deep into the abyss of the unknown and the uncomfortable places inside. Life happens, and hands us challenges to move through over and over again.

Sometimes we are moving back outward from the center of the spiral, back into a greater expression of our beautiful light and joy once again. We are expressing our gifts and feeling alive. Things are working. We are rocking it in life. And so, the cycle continues. Women are cyclical, spiraling, fluctuating creatures... not linear ones. We are always evolving, like the cycles of the moon – albeit sometimes feeling like we are moving backwards. When we are coming around the bend of that spiral again, constantly in flux and flow, we may feel like we are back to where we started or digressing, but we are always changing and rebirthing a more evolved version of ourselves if we choose to see it that way.

All of you is welcome here, your darkness and your light, the things you're proud of and the things you pray nobody ever knows... and all of the archetypes that are alive and calling within you are invited to be expressed. All of who you are is a healthy and normal part of the **Reclaim Your Power** pathway you will find in this guidebook and the accompanying programs. Here in this work, I invite you to embrace your whole, messy, brutiful (as Glennon Doyle calls it) life... and make it the best one possible.

And now it's your time to begin.

It's your time to come home to your true feminine gifts, to your authentic visions, your wisdom and your power. I know you are here on this planet for a very important reason, as we all are. Whether you are a mother, an entrepreneur, a healer, a teacher, a CEO, or an artist (and any combination of these roles or any others) – you are a CREATRIX – a powerful goddess who has the ability to create so much happiness and fulfillment in your own life, and to birth so much beauty in this world.

And this is exactly what the world needs from all of us right now.

So welcome home, Sister.

I am honored to guide you on the *Reclaim Your Power* pathway, and I thank you for entrusting me to do so. I hope it serves you as much as it has served me.

With Great Love,
Laura J. Swan

The Reclaim Your Power Invocation

Welcome to this pathway...
Called forth from deep inside of you
To reclaim what was left behind
And to remember what is True.

To say YES to your calling
To say YES to your light
To say YES to embracing the shadows
That once haunted you in the night

Because all of you is sacred
And every part of you is meant to be
And learning to embrace our wholeness
Is how we will all be set free

For this calling is to all of us
Every precious woman and girl
Because deep inside we know
That our hearts will heal the world

But first we must Remember
And Reclaim our power inside
Then Rebirth and share our gifts
With nothing left to hide

This is the path of the Awakened Woman
Where every Queen finds her truth
Your gifts need no permission
And your very existence is the proof

That you are ready for what's next
And your heart can hold it all
You are a lover, a leader,
a mother, and a light worker
Who has at last answered the call.

Chapter 1

The Reclaim Your Power Pathway

What is the RYP pathway?

The *Reclaim Your Power* pathway is a journey that I hope will inspire you to be the most whole, integrated, and powerful version of who you are meant to be in this lifetime. It is a pathway that encourages you to reclaim all parts of who you are inside, as well as discover new parts of yourself wanting to be expressed.

As I shared in the introduction, this book has a *Companion Guidebook and Creativity Journal* that goes hand in hand with the process we explore here. These materials also accompany my Reclaim Your Power program for women, which is available in an online course platform, and periodically live or in person. If you love the material we cover here, I highly encourage you to explore our guided program as well. Moving through it with like-minded women, and having the additional transformational tools and resources that the program offers, is a very unique and powerful healing experience.

As I also shared in the introduction, in this journey we move through seven different energy centers and nine different feminine archetypes, and throughout this pathway we integrate fields of archetypal psychology, feminine spirituality, art therapy, energy medicine, mythology, yoga, music, and mindset training for a holistic and multi-faceted approach.

As you can see in the graphic that follows, we will move from the ground up, from the Root Chakra to the Crown Chakra, and the nine archetypes we move through fall within this chakra system. Each archetype is built on the last one, and each energy center is activated as a result of activating the last one.

The Reclaim Your Power Pathway

The Creatrix

Crown Chakra — The Conscious Feminine Leader

Third Eye Chakra — The Wise Woman

Throat Chakra — The Queen

Heart Chakra — The Artist

Solar Plexus Chakra — The Warrioress

Sacral Chakra — The Maiden, The Lover

Root Chakra — The Mother

The Chakras and Archetypes

In the Reclaim Your Power Pathway, we travel through a series of feminine energies and archetypes. These archetypes also naturally correspond to (but are not limited to) the chakra system in energy medicine. Use this as a quick guide for the basic qualities of each archetype and the corresponding chakra qualities where they overlap.

Archetype: The Mother (Root Chakra)
Qualities: Having ultimate comfort within oneself and this world, feeling of safety in life, trust, security. Knowing you are taken care of no matter what.

Archetypes: The Maiden, The Lover
(Sacral Chakra)
Qualities: (Maiden) Newness, Playfulness, Creativity, powerful life force energy, joy, innocence and courage
Qualities (Lover): Healthy fluidity of our emotions, empowered sexuality, empowered union of masculine and feminine energies, passion, joy, vitality, sensuality and body connection (sexual or non sexual)

Archetype: The Warrioress (Solar Plexus Chakra)
Qualities: Inner power, confidence, healthy boundaries with others, fierce love, unstoppable commitment to Truth

Archetype: The Artist (Heart Chakra)
Qualities: Unconditional love, forgiveness, compassion, presence, tenderness, spaciousness, healthy balance of giving and receiving love, sharing your creative gifts and heart with the world

Archetype: The Queen (Throat Chakra)
Qualities: Speaking your truth, communicating needs to others with love, incredible self-respect, sacred self-care, inner peace through consistent, loving, empowered self-expression and voicing your truth.

Archetype: The Wise Woman (Third Eye Chakra)
Qualities: Intuition, inner wisdom, psychic abilities, accessing ancient wisdom and ancestral wisdom, deep inner guidance and truth.

Archetype: The Conscious Feminine Leader
(Crown Chakra)
Qualities: Connection to one's higher consciousness, channeling divine love and light to the world, spiritual leader and teacher, divine feminine vessel for healing on earth, values healing self to help heal the world

Archetype: The Creatrix Goddess (ALL CHAKRAS)
Qualities: The ultimate feminine power embodied; creator of beauty, love, children, and channel of life force energy and healing on earth. Infinite potential embodied, Shares her gifts openly, receives abundantly. This is the powerful creative feminine Goddess and life force energy within all of us.

Before we begin the *Reclaim Your Power* pathway, it may be useful to make sure we are on the same page here about archetypes, energy centers, and all this crazy stuff I talk about so you can understand the framework I am coming from and choosing to use for our journey together.

Why Do We Explore Mythology, Movies and Stories?

I have always loved listening to stories. Some of my most profound realizations and personal healings have come from listening to the simplest stories, even from children's books, and allowing them to penetrate to deeper places of truth within me. Mythology and stories have a way of helping us to understand complex truths and concepts inside us. They allow us to absorb ideas in a more simplified way, and these ideas can transform us from the inside out. We listen to stories and myths from a different place within us than we listen to information and facts. We listen to them often in the same way we listen to art and poetry, and open our hearts more than we would if we were studying and learning hard facts.

> *"Mythology is not a lie, mythology is poetry, it is metaphorical. It has been well said that mythology is the penultimate truth – penultimate because the ultimate cannot be put into words. It is beyond words. Beyond images, beyond that bounding rim of the Buddhist Wheel of Becoming. Mythology pitches the mind beyond that rim, to what can be known but not told."*
> ~ Joseph Campbell in *The Power of Myth*

One of my beloved mentors and teachers, who inspired much of the pathway I chose to take in my studies and my work with women, archetypes and psychology, was Dr. Anita Johnston, author of *Eating in the Light of the Moon.* Anita has touched my life in more ways than I can describe here, and the essence of her work has also become deeply infused in the essence of my work. The way she uses myths, metaphors and storytelling to teach complex concepts about feminine spirituality, body image struggles and disordered eating has been extremely powerful for me and for all the women who I refer to her work.

I invite you to let the stories, myths and metaphors I share or suggest here speak to that place within you that is beyond the mind. Listen with your inner ear and inner Wise Woman, and perhaps each archetype will come alive for you in a different way than if you were just studying the concepts alone.

What Are Archetypes?

"The contents of the collective unconscious are archetypes,
primordial images that reflect basic patterns that are
common to us all, and which have existed
universally since the dawn of time."
~ Carl Jung

The word *archetype* literally means "original pattern from which copies are made." Archetypes are forms or figures that are recurring patterns seen throughout the world, in mythology, religion, folklore stories, pop culture and more. They become the standard examples of a certain concept or idea. They embody the fundamental characteristics of something, and elicit a set of beliefs, behaviors and even emotional patterns or ways of being when we call them forth or think about them.

When I say the word "Mother," you have a basic idea and concept of what that figure and character represents. You may have your own personal life experience that influences your concept of Mother and your relationship to it, but you also have deep-seated cultural ideas of what she represents as well. Also, when I say the word Queen, or Warrioress, you will recall figures you have seen in mythology or movies, or in real life, that fall within these categories.

A belief I borrow here in this pathway from archetypal psychology is these archetypes are not somewhere outside of you, but all of them are within you. Carl Jung, Swiss psychiatrist and psychoanalyst who founded analytical psychology, taught that all of humanity shares a unified collective unconscious. All figures and forms that we see "out there" in stories or myths come from this one unified place, and therefore we can all relate to them in both a personal and collective sense.

What I believe and teach here in this work is that we all have a Queen within us. Although there is a universal idea of what the

Queen represents, we all have our own way of relating to this archetype as well. She represents regalness, poise, power and grace for many of us. She may also represent an evil, dictator, manipulative energy for some. Each archetype has both light and shadow qualities, and all of these are within us, too. The invitation in this journey is to find your own unique expression and way the archetype wants to be lived through you, and be willing to see how we embody both the shadow and light.

Each of these archetypes we explore provides an opportunity for you to activate and open parts of yourself that are elements of your own feminine energy. Some of these archetypes you may relate to, and some may feel very foreign and distant from your experience. But all have unique gifts and treasures within them. Each can provide an opportunity to learn more about different aspects of your own beautiful feminine Soul. Be curious about which ones call to you and which ones you want to run from. All of this is valuable information for your own transformational journey. Oftentimes, the ones that feel most foreign or unlike us are the ones that hold the greatest power and potential for changing our lives.

What Are the Archetypes of Feminine Power We Explore Here?
We will move through a series of 9 archetypes here: the Mother, the Maiden, the Lover, the Warrioress, the Artist, the Queen, the Wise Woman, the Conscious Feminine Leader, and the Creatrix... in that very order. Each one builds on the last, and each one

represents a world of feminine qualities, power and potential within you. I put them in this particular order with the idea that it's like we are going back in time and re-growing ourselves up again. The intention is to give the experience of moving through different stages of development as a woman one phase at a time, but this time we have the choice to do it consciously, intentionally, and with love (especially if we didn't have that experience before). These are by no means ALL of the archetypes or phases of the feminine... there are MANY more. These are the ones I have chosen that feel vital in the reclaiming of our power. Please explore the many more out there if you feel called.

> *"Shadow work is the path of the heart warrior."*
> ~ Carl Jung

We also look at both the shadow and the light of each archetype, because at any given time, both are at play in our lives and our psyches. This honest exploration allows you to face both the darkness and the light inside of you so you can honor and accept ALL of who you are as a woman, not just a small fraction of yourself that's "acceptable." We all make mistakes and behave in ways less than our full potential. Usually when we do, it is a great learning opportunity each time.

We are all human (thank goodness), and there is no part of you that is an accident or needs to be left behind. I said it before and will say it again... all of you is welcome here. And from this place of wholeness and self-acceptance, I believe you can create a life authentic to your true self, and aligned with your deepest desires and dreams.

"Wholeness is not achieved by cutting off a portion of one's being, but integration of the contraries."
~ Carl Jung

How Can We Use Archetypes for Healing, Transformation and Wholeness?

Working with archetypes, for me, is a way of reclaiming our wholeness and honoring the different parts of ourselves that want to be lived into and expressed. I believe that in modern times, women are feeling called to express ourselves and our visions for a better world in a way that is authentic to our hearts, and not depleting to our bodies. Deep inside, you may feel this and know that you too hold incredible power and potential within you to heal and change the world. And maybe you, too, feel a calling inside to rise with women worldwide and make a difference with your life.

But at the same time...perhaps you are tired from so much fighting and striving. You may ask yourself, "How am I going to help the world when I'm a hot mess myself!?" And you are not alone. We are collectively a hot mess and fed up with the way of living that requires pushing and forcing, feeling stressed and overwhelmed all the time trying to do it all.

"Healing comes from gathering wisdom from past actions and letting go of the pain that the education cost you."
~ Carolyn Myss

We are, collectively as women, ready for a new way of living and leading that encourages our wholeness and supports a way of balance in all areas of lives. In this day and age, women are living more and more multi-faceted, multi-passionate lives than ever before. But many of us are still living in an old paradigm that says we can't "have it all" unless we are exhausted and overworked. Or we are taught we have to give up a part of ourselves so that another part can thrive.

This old paradigm is disempowering to a woman's creative Soul.

Many women are choosing to be mothers and entrepreneurs (even single), or not be mothers at all, or to be corporate executives and medicine women, activists and artists...or any combination of these expressions and archetypes, and many many more... ALL AT ONCE.

In our modern times, women are DOING more than ever before. We are stepping into more and more roles, trying to balance all of it without going insane. Some are doing more as single mothers than is humanly possible! And there are many women out there who are perhaps longing for expression in certain areas of their lives, but may feel stuck and defined within one particular role.

Perhaps you are devoted to your career, and extremely efficient at what you do, but are longing for more time for your spiritual expression? More artistic or creative outlets? More connection to your body, health, and sensuality, or sexuality? Or perhaps you are a devoted mother, and fully giving of yourself to your family and children, but you are longing to be more connected to your entrepreneurial dreams or visions, your creativity and passions outside of being a mother alone?

Does this resonate for you?

If it does… perhaps it's because the truth is… all of us as women are multifaceted and incredibly complex beings. We are beautifully creative and powerfully gifted creatures, and usually long to be expressed in more than just one role or area of our lives. We long for wholeness. This is normal, and healthy, and I myself am a woman who couldn't live any other way. This is why we move through a variety of different feminine expressions – so that we can find which ones are calling to us inside and reclaim *all of who we are* to embrace our wholeness at last.

> *"To me wholeness is the key to aliveness. It's more than just physical vitality, it is radiance, coming from being at one with yourself and your experience. Life then flows through you."*
> ~ Richard Moss

Wholeness also means that, at any given time, you may unintentionally be called into a particular archetype by necessity. You may be thrust into the Warrior Goddess archetype suddenly when you lose a job and have to go out and find new work, relentlessly, to be able to provide for yourself. You may have a baby and be thrust into the Mother Archetype fully while you care for a brand new baby for a certain time period. This is also a normal and healthy tendency in life as we move in and out of different parts of ourselves that are needed to fulfill our responsibilities at the time. No one archetype defines you forever, but perhaps you may be living out the qualities and expressions of one archetype for a particular timeframe in your life. It's important to know we are fluid, changing creatures and can always create ourselves anew over and over again. Life will call forth what it needs from us, and we have a choice to trust in life each time it does.

Energy Medicine and the Chakra System

As I have mentioned, we also move through the chakra system as we go through each archetype. I will share a very basic explanation here of the chakras. If you feel called to study them further, I highly recommend looking into the resources I have provided at the end of this book.

There are seven Chakras or major energy centers, and sometimes more, depending on the energy system or tradition you are working with. The word "chakra" is derived from the Sanskrit word meaning "wheel." When you look at the literal translation from the Hindi language, it means "wheel of spinning energy." The Chakra system originated in India sometime between 1500 and 500 B.C., although some evidence suggests it goes back even further than this.

The seven Chakras are the centers in our body where energy flows, and each one corresponds to a certain color and specific collection of vibrations. They stack up our spine like a "power line" per se, all with energy meridians (like a highway system) that run throughout our entire body. The centers are connected to physical parts of the body, as well as certain emotional and spiritual patterns and belief systems. They are often depicted like a spiraling swirl and are a vortex-like powerhouse of energy in the spiritual, emotional and physical body.

> *Don't go outside your house to see the flowers.*
> *My friend, don't bother with that excursion.*
> *Inside your body there are flowers.*
> *One flower has a thousand petals.*
> *That will do for a place to sit.*
> *Sitting there you will have a glimpse of beauty*
> *Inside the body and out of it,*
> *Before gardens and after gardens.*
> ~ Kabir

Energy medicine teaches that we are all made up of energy, and to be at our best, it is important to do regular "tune-ups" or recharge our batteries and make sure our energy centers are activated and clear. Like a cell phone at the end of a day, we need to regularly recharge and balance our systems. When we don't, we feel like we don't have our full resources at our disposal.

Chakras can get blocked or out of balance because of difficult experiences, stress or trauma, and if we never do anything to help get them unstuck or back in balance, we will feel a loss of our energetic resources and just simply not be at our best. This can lead to a whole host of physical and/or emotional imbalances in the body.

As women, we need all our resources at our disposal to be at our best, and working with the chakras is one way to help sustain your energy and keep it at a healthy and balanced capacity. This pathway will offer you some basic tools and practices to realign and balance your energy centers regularly, and also help you understand what each one represents in your body, mind and spirit. If and when you feel yourself getting depleted, this will offer you some simple ways to reactivate and balance each one as we move along the pathway so you are lit up and reconnected to your full resources of power. Have fun with them and stay curious, whether they are familiar to you or you have never explored them before. See if working with them in this new way accompanied by archetypes serves you in your healing and awakening journey.

The Sacred Spiral Symbol:

The spiral symbol you see here, or as I call it the Sacred Spiral, is a symbol of the Sacred Feminine journey of remembering, reclaiming and rebirthing our true feminine power and wholeness. For me, it has come to be the symbol of the fully activated and embodied Creatrix energy (which we explore in Chapter 10), which is the infinite potential, fertility and feminine creative power that resides within all our bodies and wombs.

It also, depending on what direction you are moving inward or outward on the spiral, represents the constant cycle of evolution. We are at times moving towards darkness, endings, death and stillness (moving to the center of the spiral), then at other times, we are back into the emergence and expression of new life and brilliance (moving outward once again). It is an image of the complicated but beautiful journey of healing and transformation we experience that takes us to the center of our being... sometimes messy, sometimes feeling as if we are moving backwards or letting things fall away, but always in motion and evolving. Not in a linear way, but always in a circular, spiral motion and cycle, always transformative and rich.

"The human mind always makes progress,
but it is a progress made in spirals."
~ Madame de Stael

The spiral is also a universal symbol found throughout the world in many different ancient traditions. In fact, it is one of the oldest symbols humans have created dating back tens of thousands of years, and is also one of the most prolific and common ones.

When a symbol such as this is found all over the world in every tradition, it shows its universal significance for the human psyche and soul, and perhaps reveals a deeper, more mysterious human Soul connection than the mind can understand.

In Celtic traditions, it was thought to be a symbol of the sun and the constant radiation of infinite energy. It was also thought to represent migration and perpetual motion.

The triple spiral was said to represent the journey of the soul, from birth to death to rebirth once again. It also was used as an ancient symbol of the archetypes of the triple goddesses: the maiden, mother, and crone, and a symbol of the evolution of mysterious feminine wisdom, power and energy throughout the life cycle.

You will see the sacred spiral symbol etched onto many ancient goddess artifacts found throughout the world, symbolic of the power of a woman's fertility, and honoring her as the source of all life on this planet. In nature, you see the spiral and concentric circles everywhere, from the shape of galaxies, to the shape of shells and the center of our eyes.

I use the spiral in a lot of my programs and in my jewelry creations for this very reason. I have a special connection to it; it is a symbol for me of the inevitable truth of evolution and transformation — from the darkness to the light, and back again and again. It represents for me the divine feminine cyclical power I have come to know within my own body and Soul.

How to Get the Most Out of This Book and the Reclaim Your Power Pathway:

First of all, I invite you to have fun with this process! Stay curious and open to what is here for you. Trust that you will get exactly what you need from this experience. I recommend you read each section one by one, and take time to yourself to really reflect on the practices and journaling questions. In our online program, we work with one archetype a week and take our time to fully immerse ourselves into the energy of that archetype.

For you to fully immerse yourself in the energy of each archetype, take time to explore the myths, stories, and films suggested. Don't feel like you have to rush through each chapter. See if taking your time to move through the stories, music selections, and suggested practices, you can really tap into each unique flavor and expression of the feminine that is presented here. This level of mindfulness and spaciousness will most effectively activate the different archetypes within you.

Though of course I ALWAYS encourage you to trust your intuition and follow your inner guidance, I also believe you will get the most out of this book by following it and completing it in the order that the chapters are laid out. The archetypes are presented here as energies that are built one on top of the next.

In this *Reclaim Your Power* pathway, and from my ten-plus years of teaching about archetypes and energy medicine, I feel that the order in which I present them has been important in my students' ability to most receive each one's medicine and power. And above all... I invite you to trust in the process and see how it works for you. If it doesn't work for you or you don't resonate with it, you can always forge a new path and find your own version of it that does. I promise I will not be offended if you do. In fact, I encourage you to take what works for you here and let go of the rest. Integrate it into your own practices and philosophy and birth the most authentic path for you.

My Own Spiritual and Religious Orientation in This Work:
As you will see here in my writing, I use many different names for God. I was raised in a traditional Christian household in mid-west America, and also have Jewish roots in my matrilineal heritage. I have spent time in Israel and the Middle East diving deep into the

spirituality and religions of the region, and studied Eastern Philosophies for many years and received my B.A. in Comparative Religions and Eastern Philosophy from Boston University. I have been to the extreme of atheism and giving up on God, and I have lived in a Yogic Ashram and meditated and prayed for hours a day for months on end.

I have done my searching and looking for God everywhere "out there." In the end of all my travels, I have found a spirituality that is deeply personal and real within my own heart. I believe in a Higher Power, one that is masculine, feminine, asexual and omnipresent all in one. I am connected deeply to this Power in my life every day... and I relate to Him/Her/It in many ways... from God, to Goddess, to the Great Mystery, to Spirit, to Mother Nature, to Love.

I feel the Spirit of the Divine in all things, and yet I also have a very personal relationship with this force within my own heart. I am not any particular religion, and yet I respect and honor all religions. My invitation is for you to find your own spiritual path that feels authentic to you. All religions, paths, and practices are welcome here, and no matter your orientation, I believe you can get something valuable out of this work if you open your heart to the possibilities.

To me, more than anything, God is Love. Doing God's work in the world means aligning ourselves with Love in each moment, over our judgments and fears, and then taking action from that place in our hearts. I do my best to do God's work every day by embodying Love, compassion, and kindness in my words and actions. I certainly don't always do it perfectly, but it is my north star and the greatest intention in all I do... and it is the deepest intention of this work as well.

My Personal Stories and Embodiment of Each Archetype:

I also share within each archetype how I have personally come to understand them better. I offer you (sometimes very vulnerable) stories and experiences from my life that have influenced how I came to embody or understand each one in my own way. I don't share from a place of having mastered this work, but from a place of wanting you to see the humanness in it, and the real application of it. I am a work in progress and refining these principles and teachings within myself every day, stumbling my way through my imperfections and mistakes. As we all are.

Just as the *Reclaim Your Power* pathway is not linear but rather is more like a Spiral, the stories I tell are not linear either. I bounce around in my lifeline... so I apologize now if you get confused as to which ones happened first or when. The stories are intended to illustrate different touch points in my life where these archetypes and their corresponding qualities started to become more grounded and expressed within me. I hope these are useful and bring it home to a very real and practical place inside you.

I believe that in sharing my stories, you can better understand where I am coming from. You can better understand why this work is important to me and why I believe it can be healing for you, too. I hope the stories bring the archetypes to life for you and help you discover how to embody each one in your own way. I don't in any way expect you to express or embody them like me. I trust you will find the way that they each want and need to be activated within you. I trust with all my heart you will find your own unique expression that is beautiful and perfect for you at this time in your life.

And so, let us begin with our first story....

Storytime ~ La Loba - The Wolf Woman

I want to share a story here in the start of our journey that has always stuck with me as a metaphor for transformation and the deep healing work required for restoring and rebirthing a woman's Soul. It very much speaks to the essence of the *Reclaim Your Power* pathway, and the whole reclaiming process that we move through here. This story comes from the mountains of Northern Mexico, and I am retelling it here in my own way, and based on Dr. Clarissa Pinkola Estes version of it in *Women Who Run with the Wolves*.

La Loba, or wolf woman, is known by many names. She is said to live in the mountains and hills of Northern Mexico, and has been seen wandering the deserts from Oaxaca to El Paso and everywhere in between.

> *"The sole work of La Loba is the collecting of bones. She is known to collect and preserve especially that which is in danger of being lost to the world."*
> ~ Clarissa Pinkola Estes

La Loba collects the bones of all creatures, but she is best known for collecting the bones of wolves. She will wander and search until she has collected every last bone in order to rebuild the white skeleton of each wolf, no matter how long it may take. Each and every little bone is vital to the rebuilding of each body, and nothing must be left behind.

> *"She creeps through the mountains and the dry riverbeds, looking for wolf bones, and when she has assembled an entire skeleton, she sits by the fire and thinks about what song she will sing. Then she stands over the criatura, raises her arms over it, and sings out. Hence the rib bones and leg bones of the wolf begin to flesh out and the creature becomes furred, La Loba sings some more, and more of the creature comes into being."*
> ~ Clarissa Pinkola Estes

She takes her time to discover the song that is right for each skeleton, and sings and sings for as long as it takes to bring the creature back to life. Once the wolf has been restored, it wakes suddenly and jumps up, then runs off into the hills of the distant desert backdrop.

> *"Somewhere in its running, whether by the speed of its running, or by splashing its way into a river, or by way of a ray of sunlight or moonlight hitting it right in the side, the wolf is suddenly transformed into a laughing woman who runs free toward the horizon."*
> ~ Clarissa Pinkola Estes

And so it goes, with the bones of each wolf or creature she carefully and methodically collects, La Loba sings her song over the skeleton that was left behind, left to turn to dust in the desert, left and forgotten for good had she not reclaimed them. And with each song, she breathes new life, creativity, and love into the dried-up bones until the wild, laughing woman is reborn *and made whole, running "free toward the horizon" at last.*

Setting your Intentions for the Journey Ahead:

Now it's your turn. Take some time before we begin our journey to explore what your own intentions are at this time.

Questions for Reflection and Setting Intentions:

Now that you've read the intention of the *Reclaim Your Power Pathway*, what is your intention for yourself as you start out on this journey? What do you most want to get out of it? What is your soul most longing to experience and create at this time in your life? What are the "bones" you must collect in order to be made whole once again?

Follow your bliss.
If you do follow your bliss,
you put yourself on a kind of track
that has been there all the while waiting for you,
and the life you ought to be living
is the one you are living.
When you can see that,
you begin to meet people
who are in the field of your bliss,
and they open the doors to you.
I say, follow your bliss and don't be afraid,
and doors will open
where you didn't know they were going to be.
If you follow your bliss,
doors will open for you that wouldn't have opened for anyone else.
~ Joseph Campbell

Chapter 2

The Mother Archetype: Our Foundation of Love

Root Chakra

"A mother's love for her child is like nothing else in the world. It knows no law, no pity, it dates all things and crushes down remorselessly all that stands in its path."
~ Agatha Christie

Our journey begins with the Mother archetype. We have her here at the beginning of our pathway because she is an archetype that has such a foundational influence on how we relate to the world, as well as how we relate to ourselves. As we will explore more here, Mother is the first relationship we ever experience, even if we are adopted or raised by someone other than our own mother. We still grew as a baby in a human mother's body and related to another human for the first time as her. So much of how we see the world and take care of ourselves is connected to this archetype and these early experiences.

In this book, we explore how early experiences such as this have shaped you. The *Reclaim Your Power* pathway is one where we go back to understand and reclaim parts of ourselves from the past so that we can best bring forth who we desire to be today. So, we start with the Mother, and perhaps our youngest experience of relating to and experiencing the world, then move forward in the archetypes through different developmental stages in becoming a woman from this foundation. So let us begin…

Who Is She?

The Mother archetype energy inside us embodies unconditional love, nurturing, compassion, healing, generosity and giving. She provides a deep, safe, grounded, loving, and supportive space for others, and sees them in their wholeness and light, especially when they don't see it themselves. She has incredible patience, yet knows how to use tough love when needed. She is the fierce mama bear who makes sure her young are always protected and is willing to do whatever it takes to keep them safe. She is selflessly giving while deeply rooted and connected to the Mama Earth energy and the Great Mother energy. She sources herself from this place so that she does not burn out as she uses her resources to help and serve others.

The Shadow Side:

When out of balance, this archetype can become a martyr, overbearing or selfless to the point of losing all sense of her own needs and desires. She might be too controlling and unable to let others be their own people. She may be so identified with being "mother" that she has no other parts of herself developed, and therefore could become resentful to the world around her. She may be competitive with her offspring if she doesn't feel her own deep worth or has never lived into her own dreams and desires.

She may become neglectful of those dependent on her because she doesn't take adequate care of herself. She may also be totally absent, emotionally and/or physically, or abandoning of her children and their needs. This is not just of physical children, but also abandoning of her own creative ideas and dreams.

Why Reclaim Her?

The Mother archetype is one of the most important energies we can connect to and reclaim within ourselves. Because our relationship with our own mother was the first experience of relating and connecting to another human being, it was therefore foundational for how we relate to ourselves and all the world.

We learned how to soothe and care for ourselves by the way our mothers soothed and cared for us in our emotional, physical and spiritual needs. If this foundational relationship was empowering and supportive, we likely have a healthy connection to this archetype within us and feel capable in our own abilities to mother, care for and nurture ourselves or others.

If this relationship was wounded, didn't exist, or was challenging for whatever reason, we may not feel connected to this loving and nurturing part of ourselves, and we may not know how to deeply soothe and care for ourselves when we need it most.

When we connect to the Mother archetype, we connect to a deep and powerful part of ourselves that is independent of how we were raised. This is an energy within us and all around us of unconditional love and support, and we can always begin to cultivate and reclaim that part of ourselves no matter how old we are today. This is finding our own loving inner Mother that resides within all of us.

Through connecting to and reclaiming the Mother archetype within us, we have a chance to re-mother ourselves in a healthy and empowering way that meets our needs with care. We can learn to have deep compassion and forgiveness for ourselves and open to receive the love and nurturing that we may or may not have experienced early in life. We can also learn to best mother and care for others in a healthy and empowering way that does not deplete us of our own energy or deprive us of our own dreams.

There is a healthy balance of mothering we are looking for in this culture... one that recognizes the incredible amount of sacrifice and service that is inevitable in birthing new life (whether babies or our creative work in the world). But that also recognizes that we must not sacrifice ourselves to the point of resentment and depletion.

"If mama ain't happy, ain't nobody happy," it is said. It is vitally important that the mothers of this world feel supported by a village to nurture their children, as well as themselves.

Whatever your experience was when you were young, opening up to a relationship with this archetype within you will help you cultivate a loving, forgiving force inside you that is incredibly grounding and healing. Cultivating our own loving inner Mother, and a voice within us of compassion and care, creates a solid foundation of safety and trust that supports all we do and create in life. It also supports you to mother in a way that is most empowering for you.

When You Are Connected to Your Healthy Inner Mother:

You feel safe and rooted in your body. You trust your body and respect its cycles and changes as natural and beautiful. You trust life and know that if something goes wrong or when challenges arise, you will be there for yourself no matter what. You take care to always meet your basic needs so you are not in survival mode and do whatever it takes to get this in order. You listen to your feelings and honor them when they arise. When you are down, you nurture yourself with love and care as a loving mother would her child. You don't abandon your little girl inside or disregard her feelings, wants or desires. You forgive yourself often and can laugh at your mistakes. You are patient with yourself and others and know that no one is perfect. You respect Mother Earth and take care of her as she has taken care of you. You connect to nature regularly and source your own energy from her so you stay strong and healthy.

> *"God could not be everywhere so he created mothers."*
> ~ Jewish Proverb

Suggested Practices to Cultivate and Connect to Your Inner Mother and the Great Mother Energy:

Get connected to Mother Nature and be outside often. Go barefoot outside and get your feet on the earth. Lay belly down on the grass or on the beach and just allow yourself to do nothing as you restore your body and mind by the electromagnetic field of the earth. Breathe deeply into your lower belly and take long, slow breaths. Play African drums, or listen to African music and feel the strength in your legs as you dance. Write a letter to yourself from your loving inner Mother, perhaps with all that you wanted and needed to hear as a young girl from your own mother. Let yourself feel all that you feel as you do this, and allow the time and space for yourself to grieve, cry, laugh or celebrate the mothering experiences you had growing up. Once you write a letter from your loving inner Mother, remember to read it often, especially when you feel down or hard on yourself.

Get your hands and feet in the dirt, perhaps through gardening and growing your own food or herbs, or planting flowers. Create regular loving rituals of self-care that bring you comfort, like warm baths, cooking healthy food, enjoying gentle movement, rubbing warm oil or lotion on your body with care, and spending time with friends who love and support you. Join a women's circle and connect to the loving energy that arises from being with other women in a nurturing sisterhood support system.

"If we can ground ourselves, become one with the Earth, and treat her with care, she will nourish us and heal our bodies and minds."
~ Thich Nhat Hanh

Examples of the Mother/Mother Earth Archetype:

In Mythology and Stories:
Demeter: Mother Goddess of the harvest and fertility from Greek mythology
Mother Mary: Virgin mother of Jesus from Christianity
Isis: Goddess of fertility and motherhood from Egyptian mythology
Danu: Mother Goddess of Fertility in Irish mythology
Gaia: Ancestral Mother of all life, Mother Earth personified, Primal Mother Earth Goddess from Greek mythology
Mat Zemlya: Mother Earth Goddess from Slavic mythology
Pachamama: Ancient Fertility and Mother Earth Goddess from Inca Mythology
Nuwa: Mother Goddess of Ancient Chinese mythology

Historical or Contemporary Examples:
Mother Teresa of Calcutta
Amma: the hugging saint
Indira Gandhi: mother and Prime Minister of India
Angelina Jolie: mother, actress, and activist
Candy Lightner: founder of MADD (Mothers Against Drunk Driving)

> *"The heart of a mother is a deep abyss at the bottom of which you will always find forgiveness."*
> ~ Honore de Balzac

Affirmations to Help Reclaim Your Healthy Inner Mother:

I am safe. I am supported. I am grounded. I am loved.

I am held by the Great Mother Earth beneath me always.

I care for my heart with tenderness and compassion.

I rest my body on the Earth to be restored.

I will always be loved, supported, and taken care of... no matter what.

I trust myself to meet my needs with love and compassion.

Music to Invoke the Mother Archetype:

Ancient Mother by Robert Gass

Gaia Dreaming Herself by Deuter

I Will Be Gentle with Myself by Karen Drucker

How Could Anyone Ever Tell You by Libby Roderick

Beautiful by India Arie

Returning by Jennifer Berezan

Any earthy, deep beat **African drum music**

Storytime ~ Reclaiming My Own Inner Mother:

In my journey of reclaiming my power, this archetype was a very important and critical one for me (and is for most women), and because of this, I put her here at the beginning of our journey. When I was a young girl, my parents divorced and I lived alone with my father from age eight on. I grew up without a consistent feminine figure in my life, and this was very painful and detrimental to me as a blossoming young woman. For comfort, I turned to drugs, alcohol and boys at a very young age, and struggled with addictions of all kinds for many years trying to fill my needs for unconditional love and nurturing. I felt empty in many ways and was unable to source my own comfort and self-soothing from inside me for most of my young adult life.

At age nineteen, in the midst of a very stressful few years of college at Boston University and a time when my exercise bulimia eating disorder was peaking severely, I was called to stay in a yoga ashram in California on my summer break between sophomore and junior year. I was pulled to study yoga and practice meditating, though I knew nothing about it, and loved the idea of being in nature and the mountains of California for a couple of months.

I ended up spending the summer out there and had a profound experience of healing. While there, I for the first time heard about this idea of the "Divine Mother" essence of God, and came to experience that She was a nurturing, loving, benevolent energy who was embodied in many different sages and teachers, and ultimately... in all of creation.

I FELT her in my time here, and connected to a Mothering, loving energy that was much bigger than me, and yet inside my own heart. She was much more expansive than any physical mother could ever be, and my connection to Her was independent of what I had experienced as a young woman.

Here I was, a young Kansas girl who had never known or heard of a spirituality like this... and yet it spoke to me deeply. I felt the essence of the Divine Mother in the land all around me, and in Mother Nature and the mountains every day. I had no technology or outside contact for two months, and spent my time there in stillness, meditation, walks in nature and slowing down for the first time in my life. I listened to the voices of mountains and the trees, and I allowed myself to be fed and nourished by something other than food, addictions, sex. I started to become sourced from the inside, rather than by something outside of me, to fill my needs.

Though I still had a long healing road ahead of me, it was the first time I stopped running, literally, in my eating disorder, and my cycles of binging and purging that I had been doing for two years prior to this finally ceased. I allowed myself to be soft and patient with myself and others, like a loving mother would be with her young children, and I did gentle exercises, chanting, meditation and yoga that was nourishing to my body. I ate balanced and healthy meals, and gave myself food that was natural and pure. This was such a HUGE shift for me, as I had been so incredibly hard on myself prior to this. My time here forever gave me a reference point of inner peace that I knew was possible.

I believe this was the first time I came to understand and embody the Mother Archetype; in my time at the ashram I allowed her to hold and heal my heart. My experience of this energy was independent of something outside of me, and was certainly independent of my being able to have children myself. At this point in my life, I already had fertility problems and had been told I may never have children, so coming to know this archetypal Mothering energy within me was healing and profound. Not only because I needed it so much for myself, but I also understood it did not matter whether I had children or not... I could experience the Mother inside me, and express her fully to those around me, no matter what was true about my biology, or what was going to happen next in my life.

Questions for Reflection:

What does this archetype activate inside of you? What feelings or emotions arise? Allow some time to journal and be with all that you feel, and practice self-compassion and patience as you do. What are just a few practices you can commit to adopting to nurture yourself and activate the Mother archetype within you regularly?

The 1st Chakra: Muladhara - Root Support
Color: Red
Element: Earth
Seed Sound: Lam
Stones to Help Balance: Red Carnelian, Red Jasper

The chakra connected to the Mother archetype is the 1st Chakra, also called the Root Chakra or the Muladhara Chakra. The Root Chakra is located at the base of the spine, and is the energy center connected to your sense of physical, emotional, and spiritual safety in the world. A balanced Root Chakra leads to feeling safe, supported, grounded, and nourished by life, much like we would feel by a healthy Mothering energy.

Practice the affirmations suggested for your Root Chakra here, taking deep breaths and relaxing into your body as much as you can. The colors here you are invited to wear or surround yourself with to help balance this chakra are shades of deep red, maroon, and earthy tones of brown. Get outside, get your feet on the earth, and connect to Mother Nature often to help ground into your Root Chakra.

Root Chakra Mantras:
I am supported.
I am safe.
I am loved.

The mountains are my bones,
the rivers are my veins
The forests are my thoughts
And the stars are my dreams
The ocean is my heart
Its pounding is my pulse
The songs of the earth
Write the music of my soul

~ Unknown

Chapter 3

The Maiden Archetype: Awaken Your Joy

Sacral Chakra

"You are led through your lifetime by the inner learning creature…
the playful spiritual being that is your true self."
~ Richard Bach

We now move from the first experience of relating to the world and to what it means to be nurtured, into our first experience of relating to ourselves as young women. The Maiden archetype is the next step in our journey, and exploring her is an opportunity to reconnect to a young part of yourself in your developmental stage of womanhood. What were your first experiences of being in a young woman's body? What were you taught about your power, your voice, and your role as a woman in the world? These are all important experiences that shaped you and affected the woman you have become today. In the journey of reclaiming your power, this is an opportunity to go back to know yourself and what shaped you as a young maiden so you can understand the foundation of who you are today.

Who Is She?

The Maiden archetype is the feminine energy within us of new beginnings, excitement and the willingness to try new things. She is your youthful beginner's mind. She is the playful part of you who sees the world as one big new opportunity and place to learn and explore. She is innocence and joy, fierceness and courage. She is naive and inexperienced (sometimes in a good way) about all that could go wrong, so she is not scarred by the past or held back by fears about what may go wrong. She is the innocent part of you who has not been hurt or let down many times over, so she has nothing to be afraid of as she steps forward into her dreams. She is brave, curious, and playful, willing to make mistakes as she steps into her new life and new opportunities. She is light, magical and fun. She has a magnetic and charismatic energy about her that draws people in, invites them to play, and encourages them to smile and take life less seriously. She is independent and yet always excited and eager to make new friends and meet new people. She trusts life and sees it as an expression of the magical, fantastic world inside her.

The Shadow Side:

When your inner Maiden is out of balance, or is not being expressed or cultivated regularly, you may feel shut down and rigid, or perhaps you may be told by others that you are "no fun anymore" or "need to lighten up."

When your inner Maiden is not cultivated and empowered in a healthy way (either in youth or as an adult), she may also have fears about not ever being enough or not having enough experience. She may be scared to put herself out there because she doesn't feel like anyone will listen or care. She has no confidence in new situations or circumstances.

The disempowered Maiden voice says, "I'm too young, I'm not experienced, I'm not relevant, there are so many more people out there older/more experienced than me, I'm scared of new places and can't handle it alone. I need someone to hold my hand." This disempowered Maiden voice is the part of us that was never given the confidence to believe in herself. But the good news is, it is never too late to remember her gifts and beauty now.

There is also the flip side of the imbalanced inner Maiden that rebels against all authority, and may say, "I don't have to listen to ANYONE or ANYTHING and I'm going to do whatever I want" (in more of a rebellious, reckless, bratty way). She is not willing to receive help or guidance to a fault, and can cause a lot of problems in her relationships by being too self-centered and unwilling to see other people's perspectives. She may be unable to see how her behavior is impacting others, and therefore creates chaos and destruction rather than connection. She may be too absorbed in play and not enough in fulfilling her responsibilities in life, or may simply have no grasp on how to be responsible at all.

This shadow side of the maiden emerges because she was never empowered to be responsible or self-sufficient in a healthy way. She wasn't taught what it means to believe in herself and trust her own inner guidance and heart.

Why Reclaim Her?

For many women, we have lost touch with this playful and joyful part of ourselves and can fall into patterns of rigidity and stress easily as adults. We get caught up into believing that life is always so serious, which leads to feelings of anxiety, depression and overwhelm and a focus on what we need to produce rather than on the joy of being alive.

We can understandably lose touch with our healthy Maiden self for many reasons in our culture. To name just a few reasons: we think we have to grow up and lose our playfulness to become successful, or we had difficult experiences when we were maidens ourselves, or we experienced trauma as a young girl. This vital and playful part of ourselves may have been left far behind in the past because it is not remembered as a happy time for us.

As adults, we can reclaim this part of ourselves and bring her back into our lives in a healthy way so we can awaken to our full joy once again. We can even go back in time to remind our youthful self just how precious and powerful she was then and still is today (see journaling exercises below).

Reclaiming your inner Maiden will help you to connect and trust her gifts more fully within yourself now as an adult, and will allow her to have a place to play and be expressed in your life today.

When You Are Connected to Your Inner Maiden:

When connected to your inner Maiden, the world looks bright and hopeful. You are magnetic to the world and others, because joy and playfulness are alluring and attractive in all ways. You don't take things too seriously, and even things that are serious and heavy you can hold onto with a light heart.

You are courageous and willing to try new things and genuinely curious about new opportunities ahead. In business, leadership, and life, this can be a very valuable archetype to call forth to move forward in your dreams and visions without fear debilitating you – paralyzing you – with all the reasons why you shouldn't take action. In her healthy expression, she has a valuable naivety and fearlessness to call forth so you can GO FOR IT, and have fun along the way.

She is also precious medicine to call forth if you have trouble letting go of stress and lightening up; she helps you to loosen your rigid grip on life when things seem very serious. She is a wonderful energy to call forth when you need to just relax and see the world or your problems through a different perspective and you need a little joy, play, and fun in your day (which we ALL do regularly!). When you need to lighten up and let go of control... the Maiden is your girl.

> *"We don't stop playing because we get old,*
> *we get old because we stop playing"*
> ~ George Bernard Shaw

Suggested Practices to Cultivate and Connect to Your Inner Maiden:

Get outside, breathe fresh air and get sunshine regularly, surround yourself with colorful flowers and bright colors in general. Put flowers in your hair, daydream and watch the clouds go by. Look for fairies and magic everywhere, skip instead of walk, play in the forest, park, or at the beach, lay in the grass, go barefoot. Focus on BEING and enjoying the moment rather than DOING and being productive. Take a day or afternoon off and have a date with your Maiden self to do whatever she wants to do (go to the movies, get ice cream, go bowling, visit the arcade, toy store, or take a slow, wandering nature walk). Do something courageous and new just for the sake of doing it with no attachments to the outcome. Try laughing yoga. Write a letter to your inner

Maiden and tell her how precious and beautiful she is… how much you respect and admire her, and if it feels authentic, how sorry you are if she never learned this from the world around her in her youth. Let her know it is never too late to play again, and you are here for her now.

> *"Why, sometimes I've believed as many as six*
> *impossible things before breakfast."*
> ~ Alice in *Alice in Wonderland*
> by Lewis Carroll

Examples of the Maiden Archetype:

In Mythology, Movies, and Stories:
Annie in *Annie* (1982)
Merida in *Brave* (2012)
Moana in *Moana* (2016)
Alice in *Alice in Wonderland*
Anne in *Anne of Green Gables*
Laura in *Little House on the Prairie*
Persephone: Goddess of the Underworld, Youth, and Fertility in Greek Mythology
Idunn: Goddess of Youth in Norse Mythology
Ostara: Goddess of Spring in Germanic Mythology

Historical or Contemporary Examples:
Shirley Temple: famous child actress
Dakota Fanning: American child actress
Ellen Degeneres: comedian, talk show host, actress
Cameron Diaz: American actress
Dolly Parton: singer/songwriter
Drew Barrymore: American actress
Gwen Stefani: singer, songwriter
Camille Macres: creator and founder of Camille's Paleo Kitchen

"Being playful is a great emotional resource."
~ Dr. LaCombe

Affirmations to Reclaim Your Inner Maiden:
I play and dance with life each day.
Every day is a chance to explore my world.
All my dreams are coming true!
I can create and do anything my heart desires!
I take on the world today and try new things.
I'll never give up no matter how many times I fall down.
I am brave and courageous.
I can do anything!

Music to Invoke and Empower Your Inner Maiden:
Beautiful Flower by India Arie
I'm Just a Girl by No Doubt
New Soul by Yael Naim
Girls Just Wanna Have Fun by Cyndi Lauper
Run the World (Girls) by Beyonce
How Far I'll Go by Auli'i Cravalho - from Disney's *Moana*
Soundtrack

Storytime ~ How I Reclaimed My Inner Maiden:
I moved to San Diego when I was around 23 years old to work and live as a Nutritional Therapist and Gerson Therapy caregiver, which means I was a practitioner of an all-natural healing treatment for cancer (and for many other diseases and illnesses). In that time, I also enrolled in a Holistic Health Practitioner (HHP) program and was in psychotherapy myself, which started to uncover some deeper layers of healing I needed to do around my childhood and past.

I discovered in this time that at a very young age, I had stopped being playful and free, and had to become an adult overnight when my parents split. Living alone with my father and older sister from age eight on, I had to learn how to do laundry, cook, clean, and take care of myself pretty quickly. And all of this while also feeling the heartbreak of my family falling apart. At a very young age, I was comforting my dad who was struck with debilitating grief and pain without my mother around. I became a caregiver very young, and forgot what it meant to be a child. I started my menstrual cycle by age ten, started using drugs and alcohol by age eleven, and started engaging in sex and boys by age thirteen.

In many ways, I lost my childhood innocence and my sense of joy very young, and here at age twenty-four in the midst of my own personal healing, I realized I needed to go back and reclaim her and give that little girl a chance to live inside me once again. I was so serious all the time and had an intensity and stress level that was not healthy, even though I appeared calm and centered on the outside. I had done a lot of healing work on myself, but I still was not happy. My inner maiden had been hiding, still holding onto a lot of pain and sadness, and had been lost many years ago behind my need to be "grown up" far too fast.

At age twenty-four I decided I was going to invite her out to play again. I started doing some inner-child healing work between my HHP program and with my therapist, and had a couple of month time period where I felt like I was almost constantly a playful little girl again (while still living and working as an adult... that was interesting). And though it was very foreign at first, it felt so good. Each day, I asked my inner maiden, my little girl inside, what SHE wanted to do in addition to what my adult self had to accomplish each day. I wore dresses and pigtails a lot. I skipped more. I had play dates and took myself to the park to lay in the sun and enjoy the breeze without any agenda. I smelled flowers every time I passed them. I colored a lot.

And more than anything, I reclaimed a part of myself that had been buried down deep for a very long time. I gave her permission to have a place in my life, and felt the shift and change in my experience of joy and love every day. I consistently made the effort to be less serious and PLAY more. Eventually my inner Maiden became a natural part of me once again without having to try so hard to bring her forth each day.

I still have to make the effort to consciously invoke her often, especially when I get too serious or work too hard (which is often). Especially now that I have a little maiden daughter of my own, I realize even more the importance of not taking myself so seriously and allowing myself to just BE FREE and in JOY as often as I can with her. When I'm not... my relationship with her suffers, and I can feel it. With all of the roles and responsibilities we hold as women, I have come to discover that this playful part of me is vital to my health and happiness, as well as to my connection with my family and children every day.

Questions for Reflection:

What feelings are activated inside you through exploring this archetype? How is your own inner Maiden longing to be expressed or reclaimed? What are a few practices you can commit to in order to help encourage your Maiden to come out and play more?

The 2nd Chakra: Svadhisthana - Sacral Chakra
Color: Orange
Element: Water
Seed Sound: Vam
Stones to Help Balance: Orange Carnelian,
Orange Moonstone, Coral

The chakra connected to the Maiden Archetype is the 2nd Chakra, also called the Sacral Chakra or the Svadhisthana Chakra. The 2nd Chakra is located above the pubic bone and below the navel, and encompasses the genital region and the hypogastric plexus. It is connected to your creativity, playfulness, pleasure, and sexuality. We'll go more into the sensual and sexuality aspects of this chakra next in the Lover archetype… for here we are focusing on the play, joy, spontaneity, and pleasure aspects that are more connected to the Maiden archetype.

A balanced 2nd chakra creates a sense of freedom in the body, playfulness, and courage to be yourself, relate to others, and take risks, much like a brave young Maiden who has been taught her true power. Practice the suggested mantras here, and if you'd like, you are invited to wear bright shades of orange (think of a sunrise or sunset) to help activate and balance this energy. Have fun and let your creative, carefree Maiden come out to play as you do this.

Sacral Chakra Mantras:
I am Playful.
I am Free.
I am Alive.

"Being playful naturally liberates the mind,
opens the heart,
and lifts the spirit.
Take time to play today"
~ Debra L. Rebie, PhD

Chapter 4

The Lover Archetype: Come Home to Your Body

Sacral Chakra

"The body is an instrument which only gives off music when it is used as a body. Always an orchestra, and just as music traverses walls, so sensuality traverses the body and reaches up to ecstasy."
~ Anais Nin

Next we move into the Lover archetype. Ideally, a young Maiden becomes a young woman in a healthy and empowered way, and comes to understand that her body is sacred and precious. She enters into her sexuality with non-judgment, and gets to know what brings her pleasure from a place of curiosity and joy. Unfortunately, this is not usually the norm in our culture. The Lover archetype is the next step in our journey because she represents how we relate to our bodies and our sexuality, how we relate to others through our bodies, and how we receive and take in pleasure in all ways... sexual and non-sexual. This relationship with our sexuality is shaped also very young, either as teens or in our early 20's, or sadly it can become shaped through negative or traumatic sexual experiences as well. In reclaiming our power, we go back to our early experiences of what shaped us, and reclaim the relationship we want to have with our bodies today from a place of love and empowerment.

Who Is She?

The Lover archetype is sensual, open, receptive, passionate, and delighted by the pleasures all around her. She drinks in the sweet nectar of life and enjoys and celebrates her body as a sacred temple to both give and receive pleasure and love. She enjoys touch, closeness and intimacy. She is alluring, seductive and empowering. She experiences ecstasy, joy, creativity and playfulness, and invokes these qualities in those around her by her very presence. She is comfortable in her sexuality and celebrates it with respect. She feels safe in her body because she respects it with love and care, and ensures that others do, too.

She considers the union of masculine and feminine energy to be one of life's most sacred gifts when it is chosen from an empowered place for all involved. She loves deeply, openly and actively, and seeks out love and connection with others in a healthy, beautiful way. The archetype has many different faces, and you may relate to some or all of them. She may also be expressed as the partner, spouse, seductress, enthusiast or sacred prostitute. She sees beauty everywhere; she takes in the beauty all around her and is delighted by the ecstasy of life.

The Shadow Side:

If the Lover archetype energy within us is out of balance, she can depend entirely on attention, physical affection and pleasure from the outside to fill her. She becomes obsessive and addicted to love and affection at the detriment of her own health and sanity. She can source all of her self-worth from other people's acceptance and reassurance, rather than from her own inner resources. She may put all the value of her self-image into her physical appearance, and therefore put an imbalanced amount of time and energy into her looks and beauty.

She may take pride in her ability to seduce or please others, but come to rely fully on physical expressions of love and sexuality rather than on her own spiritual connection to her inner truth and beauty. She can use her beauty and magic to seduce others in a negative, manipulative way rather than an empowering, consensual way for all involved. She can lose connection to herself and her deepest desires for authentic love. She can feel shame about her sexuality and her body and disconnected to what brings her pleasure, either because of cultural learning or traumatic experiences around her body and sexuality.

Why Reclaim Her?

Many of us as women are never taught how to have a healthy relationship with our bodies, let alone our sensuality and sexuality. Unfortunately, there are far too many of us as women who have experienced sexual trauma, abuse or rape, and have disconnected from the body entirely because it does not feel like a safe place to be. Reclaiming the Lover archetype within can help us to reconnect to a beautiful, sensual part of ourselves as a woman... one that is vital for our well-being and creativity, and one that can never, ever be taken away from us.

We are, by nature, sensual creatures and get so much joy and pleasure from BEING in our bodies when we can allow ourselves to be present in them and drop our judgments. Much easier said than done, right? And that is why we hold this intention here of reclaiming her. In doing so, we allow ourselves to wash away and surrender the years of accumulated judgments and criticisms of our bodies. We begin to tap into the truth of their magic and beauty when we touch upon our inner Lover and start loving ourselves and our physicality in a whole new and empowering way.

We also often make sensual mean sexual, and though it certainly can be connected, they are not always connected. Tapping into our body's sensuality on a regular basis, and allowing ourselves to receive the beauty and pleasures of being in a human body, is one of life's greatest gifts. And as women, many of us have become disconnected from this powerful and precious gift of our bodies. Many women experience sex with no sensuality or deep fulfillment, or rigidity in our movement or life, or feel disconnected to our bodies altogether, or criticize and make our bodies wrong because they don't look "perfect" according to some artificial external definition of what that means.

The Lover archetype is fluid, free, flowing, and does not allow herself to be defined by the outside. She connects to her body and soul's DESIRE from the inside and follows it and trusts it with all her being. She drops the shame around feeling sexual and sexy, and owns it with confidence. She owns her sexual desires and fantasies, whatever they may be, and as healthy and good... not weird or perverted. She accepts all her sexual self in her wholeness, wounds from the past and all.

When we can reconnect to this part of ourselves, a part that is defined by our own sense of what FEELS good in our bodies, rather than what we think the world wants from us, we are reclaiming a very powerful energy within us. We are less dependent on cues from the outside from others, and instead listen deeply to the voice of our body on the inside. From this place, we become much more connected to our sexual lovers or romantic partners because we know our own bodies and we respect ourselves. We are much more open and receptive to a deep, meaningful, connected interaction with others from this place.

This is very important to the Lover, to be connected in an intimate, rich, and meaningful way with others, both sexually and non-sexually.

On the flip side, many of us as women may be so over-identified with the imbalanced Lover inside that we feel all our worth depends on our sexuality and what we give others. Reclaiming the empowered, healthy Lover within you is a way of reclaiming your sexual sovereignty, recognizing the power and beauty inside you is not dependent on your sexuality, and respecting this gorgeous gift of your body that you have with all your heart. It is a way of reclaiming our bodies as precious and recognizing that we have a right to say who gets to experience them and who doesn't. This is vitally important in reclaiming our power as women.

When You Are Connected to Your Healthy Inner Lover:
You feel free in your body and flowing in your life. You respect your body and allow it to go through cycles and phases of age, weight, sickness and different physical expressions without making it wrong or judging it. You find joy by being present in the world and look for beauty all around you. You are magnetic, charismatic and playfully flirtatious when you want to be. You allow yourself to feel DESIRE in a big way and don't shrink back from its power. You release shame from your body and allow yourself to fully enjoy pleasures without guilt. You OWN your sexy self. You take in compliments and can receive attention without feeling unworthy. You know you are a damn HOT MAMA, no matter your size, shape, or age. You own your natural, inherent beauty without makeup or dressing up... as well as you love to adorn and dress yourself up as a goddess when you see fit. You have fun with your

clothing and adornments, you enjoy color and creativity and allow this to be an art and joy rather than burden. You delight in flavors, sounds, touch and all stimulation of the senses, and you are grateful for the beautiful gift of being in a body every day.

> *"The touch of the sea is sensuous, enfolding the*
> *body in its soft, close embrace."*
> ~ Kate Chopin

Suggested Practices to Cultivate and Connect to Your Inner Lover:

Allow your body to be caressed by nature, feel the breeze on your skin, enjoy the sensation of warm water on your naked body in the bath or swimming, feel warm sun on your face and soak it in. Taste life fully, enjoy food slowly, experience a variety of flavors to stimulate your palate, let food be both medicine and pleasure. Practice pure presence and being in the moment… your senses are most fed by experiencing the here and now. Find what you are passionate about, deeply and truly, and give yourself the gift of enjoying your passions regularly. Dance in a way that makes you feel free in your body: belly dance, hula hoop, pole dance, learn how to lap dance. Move in any way that makes you feel good and connects you to your fluid, strong and sexy body. Get to know your body and what makes you feel sexually turned on through self-pleasuring or with a partner. What REALLY turns you on? Claim it and be proud of it… and take time to explore, be curious and learn about your body. And then be brave to ask for what your body loves and wants. Know that you deserve to receive the most beautiful pleasure possible. Every day ask yourself... What do I DESIRE today? And then indulge in AT LEAST one pleasurable desire each day that nourishes your Lover inside.

> *"Dance is the hidden language of the soul of the body."*
> ~ Martha Graham

Examples of the Lover Archetype:

In Mythology, Movies, and Stories:
Aphrodite: Goddess of Love, Beauty, and Sexuality in Greek Mythology
Inanna: Sumerian Goddess of the Moon, Fertility, and Sexual Love
Mary Magdalene: Though not traditionally a Goddess, she holds an archetypal power of sacred sexuality and the high priestess for many women
Lilith: Dark goddess of the Hebrew faith, represents female sexual empowerment
Juliet in *Romeo and Juliet*
Rose (Kate Winslet) in *Titanic* (1997)

Historical or Contemporary Examples:
Elizabeth Taylor: British-American actress, businesswoman, and humanitarian
Marilyn Monroe: actress, model
Madonna: singer, songwriter
Scarlett Johansson: actress, writer, model
Jena La Flamme: author and founder of Pleasurable Weight Loss
Roxanne DePalma: pole dance fitness instructor, co-founder of PlayDen Productions
Elizabeth DiAlto: speaker, author, and creator of the Wild Soul Movement

"Never be ashamed of passion. If you are strongly sexed,
you are richly endowed."
~ Margaret Sanger

Affirmations to Help Reclaim Your Healthy Inner Lover:

It is safe to love and be loved by another.

I open myself to receive the joys and pleasures of my body.

I experience love and beauty every day.

I speak my desires with confidence and trust.

I allow pleasure in my life in all ways.

My body is sacred, sexy, and sensual in my unique way.

I listen to and honor the desires of my body.

Music to Invoke the Lover Archetype:

Feeling Good by Nina Simone

Afterglow (featuring Soundmouse) by Phaeleh

Bad Karma by Axel Thesleff

Crave You (Adventure Club Remix) by Flight Facilities

Private Party by India Arie

Closer by Nine Inch Nails (an edgy one here... be aware of adult language and content)

Storytime ~ How I Reclaimed My Own Inner Lover:

I first want to say that I know what I'm about to share may be quite controversial. I have shared this story up to this point in limited and safe places, and I am aware of how triggering and difficult it may be for some. However, regardless of your moral stance on this issue, I know how much pain so many women, including myself, have held inside as a result of unplanned pregnancies and abortions. So, I'm not willing to keep my story a secret or hidden out of fear of being judged or criticized. It's a part of me, and of so many woman, and has partially shaped who I am.

I have realized that no matter how much judgment I may receive from the outside, it could not compare to the judgment I had to face within myself around my past. And I believe that once we truly face this self-judgment, and transform it into love, the criticism from the outside can no longer debilitate us. I have become committed in this lifetime to a path of self-compassion, fully releasing the shame and guilt in my body from past mistakes or choices. I hope in sharing this story, it will help you to do the same.

In my twenties, I went through a time of completely shutting down to my body, and to my sexuality and sensuality as a woman. I had been very sexual as a teen, though I was ashamed of it and tried to hide it, often out of concern for what it would do to my reputation and out of fear of being seen as a "slut." I experienced both intense highs and intense challenges as a result of my sexuality, and yet it was a part of me that probably saved my life after my family fell apart so young.

When I discovered sex, I felt a closeness, affection and pleasure I had never known, and it came at a very critical time in my troubled years after the sadness and loss of my family. Of course, I equally discovered heartache and pain around sex, as I soon realized that not every guy I had sex with in those early years was in it for love and connection. My teenage years were a mixed relationship with sex, but ultimately, even though I wouldn't admit this to the world around me, I was a very sexual person as a young woman and felt highly connected to my body.

But things slowly started to change. After a series of three unplanned pregnancies, followed by complicated, challenging abortions at sixteen, seventeen and eighteen, I completely shut down to my body and my sexuality. I felt that if sex was going to cause so many problems and heartaches, it wasn't worth having it ever again. And my body became a place of shame, pain, and guilt... not of pleasure any longer.

Having an abortion in Kansas was not a simple thing at that time. I was surrounded with pro-life billboards and propaganda everywhere I went, and I felt I had to hide what I was going through from my parents and most of the people in my life. I was terribly ashamed and embarrassed about my first pregnancy, let alone the two that followed, and felt more and more guilty each time. But I couldn't let go of sex because it had become my main source of love and connection so young. It caused a lot of problems, but who was I without it?

I was on the pill to avoid pregnancy, but I was clearly so incredibly fertile that any slip up on taking my pills, missing one day, a condom breaking, taking medication that affected it and so on, would result in a pregnancy. I was so set on going to college and following a certain path of success that I could not fathom having a baby at that age, even though deep in my heart I desperately longed to become a mother one day. Finally, after the third abortion, I said enough. I shut down to my sensuality completely, vowed to never have sex again, and went away to college at Boston University shortly after. I felt shame around choices I had made and ways I had let myself down, but I wasn't able to understand that so young, so I internalized all of it. And so began my journey into deep depression, sadness, and severe anxiety that lasted for a few years.

While at BU, things spiraled downward fast. I hated my body by this time, as it had become a war zone for me rather than a place of pleasure. Subconsciously I must have wanted to disappear completely and didn't want to attract any attention or sexual advances at all. I stopped having my menstrual cycles and developed deep self-hatred, judging myself harshly for all my mistakes and pain from the past. I developed an eating disorder in this time called exercise bulimia, which meant that I would eat very few calories each day, and whatever I did eat, I was sure to run enough miles to burn above and beyond any calories I had consumed. At my peak, I was running eight to nine miles and eating around 500 calories a day.

I got down to around 90-95 pounds and felt absolutely no sex drive or connection to my body whatsoever. Any attempts at being sexual by choice were an abysmal failure, and in my sophomore year I had a traumatic sexual experience that caused me to shut down even further. I was withering away, studying constantly, working three jobs, and pushing myself beyond my limits so that I didn't have to stop and feel any pain from the present or past. I stopped having sex for some time, not from a place of confidence and empowerment, but rather from the intensity of my guilt and fear around it.

Fast forward to my time in Hawaii... (the story of how I got there from Boston you'll read in Chapter 8). When I arrived in Hawaii to spend a year living and working on the Big Island, I was broken. I was thin, frail, depressed, and coming off my years of hard pushing at BU. But something magical started to happen in my time there. Just as Mother Nature had started to heal me at my time in the ashram the summer prior to this, I felt her power in Hawaii once again. Hawaii is a place of pure beauty and pleasure, and every sight, sound and taste is an orgasm for the senses. But I was so shut down in my body that it took me a few months to receive it and to finally let life in once again.

After a few months there, I started to feel the magic of the land working on me. I felt myself softening inside and listening to my body more and more. I started frolicking in the warm ocean waters like a mermaid, and made a habit of swimming with wild spinner dolphins in the bays almost every day. The dolphins, and all these precious elements of nature, brought me back to life again. I tried belly dancing for the first time out there, and danced under the full moons with a circle of gorgeous, voluptuous goddesses by my side. I started to eat delicious tropical fruit, freshly caught fish and juicy ripe avocados growing on the trees outside my front door.

Slowly, I started to connect to a Higher Power of Love inside and all around me again like I had at the ashram. Slowly I started to forgive and be gentle with myself and my body, one breath at a time. I started to take in the beauty from this magical land to allow my body to be opened to joy and life once again, and I let myself receive pleasure at last, though this time it was not sexual, but deeply sensual on all levels. It was slowly... I emphasize that strongly here. I did not make changes overnight, but this place began to open and heal me over time.

After some time of reconnecting to my sensuality independent of men and sex, I eventually met a young man out there who became my boyfriend. He gently and beautifully helped me open up again to my sexuality. I would not have sex with him for the first several months we were together and told him to never expect it unless we got married.

But as I slowly healed, started to forgive myself and open up again, I consciously decided that I was ready again. This time it was from a conscious choice and a place of empowerment, rather than from an unconscious desire to fill a hole in my heart.

I wanted to feel safe in my body again and enjoy the pleasure of my sexuality... but it had been so long since I had allowed that. In my time in Hawaii, my boyfriend was patient and loving, and I would try sometimes to be sexual, and then take a few steps back in my progress. Ultimately with time and love, I came to trust my body again and release some of the shame that had crippled me for years. I felt loved by the land, the creatures, the people, my partner, and I learned to love and forgive myself in a much deeper way.

In this time in Hawaii, I started a new level of healing with my body that continued for many years to come. It was in that place I learned I could make love to life once again. I learned to embrace my healthy inner Lover from a place of power and self-love and to see my sexuality as a sacred gift once again. Hawaii will forever be in my heart and Soul as a result of the transformation that I experienced there. I still had a long road of healing ahead, but the progress there around my sexuality, my fertility, and my body was a miracle for me.

When I share this story with the women I know, love, and work with, I have found that about 75% of them admit they had abortions too, and of that, a large percentage of them have either told no one at all or told very few people because of the shame they feel. There is no set way in our culture to deal with the pain of abortions or pregnancy losses of any kind, and the judgment in the world around these areas can be intense and cruel at times. It's my desire to support all women who suffer with these losses or traumatic sexual experience to heal and transform the guilt, pain, and shame at last. So, I share this story with you now from a place of love, and a desire to help set us all free from the pain and guilt that so many, many women carry in our bodies around our sexuality and past. I believe, with all my heart, we truly can be free.

Questions for Reflection:

What feelings or emotions are activated inside you through exploring this archetype? Have you also held onto shame or pain from your past? What experiences from your past would you like to release from your body and forgive yourself for at last? Take some time as you reflect to imagine yourself free from self-judgment or shame around the past, and see how that feels in your body. What practices here will you commit to taking on to awaken your healthy inner Lover?

The 2nd Chakra: Svadhisthana
Color: Orange/Hot Pink
Element: Water
Seed Sound: Vam
Stones to Help Balance: Orange Carnelian,
Pink Moonstone, Coral

We stay within the 2nd Chakra, the Sacral Chakra, for the Lover archetype because of the connection to passion, play, and sensuality that the 2nd chakra represents. A healthy 2nd chakra will create a sense of safety in exploring your sensuality and sexuality, and when balanced you feel creative, passionate, and alive with life force energy. In the Lover, we focus on these aspects of the second chakra, so feel free to play with wearing or surrounding yourself with shades of orange again or hot pink to help bring out the hotness of your inner Lover. Think about the colors of a gorgeous sunrise or sunset again, now with bright pink hues… these are your colors here.

And practice the affirmations for the Lover archetype while you indulge in some fresh juicy fruit, chocolate, or something special and delicious for your taste buds. Be present with this process, connected to each bite, sound, or sensation, and even take in through your eyes the beauty of the colors of each food or object around you. Play one of the suggested songs, and maybe even start dancing with your sexy self (or for someone else) if you feel so inclined.

Sacral Chakra Mantras:

I am sensuous.

I am passionate.

I create from pleasure.

"The world is little, people are little, human life is little. There is only one big thing — desire."

~ Willa Cather

Chapter 5

The Warrioress Archetype: Activate Your Fierce Love

Solar Plexus Chakra

"The more you are motivated by love, the more fearless and free your actions will be."
~ The Dalai Lama

The next stop in our journey of empowerment is the Warrioress archetype. After we connect to the relationship that we developed with our bodies and our sexuality in the Lover, we come to understand our relationship with our inner power, strength, and inner resilience. The Warrioress archetype represents how we put ourselves out there and create what we want to manifest in the world. She also represents the masculine energy within us, which often gets shaped by our first experience of men. For many women this is our fathers, but not always. So as the Mother is our first experience of the feminine energy within us, the Warrioress is the first exploration of the father or masculine energy within us. It is an opportunity to look at how you came to know this energy in the world, as well as how you hold both masculine and feminine energy within you. This is a divine union that we need in order to create a life we desire from a place of wholeness. Reclaiming your inner power, healthy masculine energy, and Warrioress supports stepping into the woman you want to be in the world, and manifesting a life most authentic to your heart.

Who Is She?

The Warrioress, also called the Warrior Goddess, energy inside you is a fierce protector of all that she holds as sacred, and she allows nothing to get in her way. She is confident, powerful, and determined and knows when it's time to be relentlessly devoted to a cause or a goal. She holds a balance of masculine action and feminine heart and is able to execute effectively on her visions and ideas. She has single-pointed focus and can carry a task through from start to finish without falling prey to distractions. She does not fight for the sake of fighting, but only for the greatest and highest good of love and truth. She executes her goals and is relentlessly committed to her visions and dreams. She is assertive and doesn't let others intimidate her with their words or energy. She triumphs against all odds, even when it seems she is defeated. She is incredibly strong, resilient, and an unstoppable force for the ultimate and highest good for herself and the world. Fierceness is her guide and love is her superpower. She is able to hold strong but healthy boundaries between herself and others and move through the world with confidence and grace because of this. She is not afraid to destroy or let die what is no longer serving the highest good so that the truth can emerge in its place.

The Shadow Side:

When out of balance on overdrive, the Warrioress energy can go too far into her masculine driven energy. When on overdrive, she doesn't know when to stop and allow her soft feminine energy to take the lead, or when to allow time for rest and rejuvenation. She sees only the end goal, with no mercy, and forgets to sustain her energy along the way. She gets burned out and depleted. She is staying active and in execution mode out of a need to feel busy or important or needing a distraction from feeling her feelings. This is rather than taking action out of inspiration and devotion to a cause or purpose. When she is all action and drive, she doesn't know how to RECEIVE or rest in her feminine.

On the flip side, when we are not allowing the Warrioress to be expressed at all, the other end of the spectrum is that we feel stuck in inaction with all vision and no inspired action to manifest our goals and dreams. We may not know what to "do" or feel overwhelmed by any task that requires commitment, because we feel afraid of not being able to follow through consistently. Or we simply don't want to do the work it takes. We could also perhaps be afraid of how strong we really are and do not unleash our fierceness or shy away from it because it is so powerful. We may not have fully claimed our true feminine power because it was never cultivated as a young girl or it was squashed or discouraged instead. If we don't feel connected to our own intensity and inner power, we may also fear we can't protect ourselves from other people's energy or intense situations, so we avoid intensity all together.

Why Reclaim Her?

The Warrioress energy within us is a potent and powerful force to help move our dreams and visions forward. Often, we as women either have this energy on overdrive or dormant, and finding the balance of the Warrioress in our lives is where we find our special magic to make things happen. She represents the healthy masculine drive within us, and when in touch with her, we can move our visions and intentions forward with consistency, courage and clarity. She is the single pointed focus within us, which can be very hard for some women. We can follow through on a task from start to finish and fulfill on our commitments we care most about. So many of us as women have incredible feminine gifts of love, compassion, healing, and tenderness to share… but may not be in touch with the drive within us to bring those gifts to the world in a consistent, impactful and lucrative way (if that's what we desire to do).

The Warrioress energy gets s*** done and makes sure that this beautiful, feminine energy that you hold inside has the freedom and spaciousness to flow and do her magic in the world. She is the side of you that fiercely protects your sensitivity and softness so it does not have to be hidden from the world. When we reclaim the Warrioress inside of us, it's like we are unleashing our inner fierce protector of our own beautiful gifts and of our deepest truth and tenderness inside.

Being in touch with this part of ourselves helps to ensure that we are a healthy blend of vision and action. When she is activated and allowed to be in her full power, there is a divine marriage of masculine/feminine energy inside us that is supportive of both our "being" and our "doing," both of which are necessary to have balance in life every day.

When this divine marriage of masculine/feminine energy is happening within us, we are also much more likely to be able to manifest this healthy divine marriage in our outer world. To be in touch with, but not over-identified with, our healthy Warrioress and masculine drive helps us to attract a healthy masculine energy in our partnerships and romantic relationships too.

"Knowing what must be done does away with fear."
~ Rosa Parks

When You are Connected to Your Healthy Inner Warrioress:
You are charismatic, powerful, and strong... without being overpowering of others. You feel safe in the world because you know you will hold healthy boundaries with others. You don't let others treat you with disrespect because you love and respect yourself fiercely. You feel committed to a cause, any cause, that

gets you fired up...whether it be the values of love and kindness in the world, conscious parenting or fighting for the rights of those less fortunate, like refugees or at-risk youth. You fight for the right to be yourself, against all odds, and you protect your inner little girl with fierce love (because that's what she deserves). You move your dreams forward, every day, and you don't let anyone else tell you what you can and can't accomplish. You may get knocked down, over and over, but you get right back up... and begin again. Your power is sourced from within you and from God, and you know who you are and what magnificent gifts you hold inside. In general, you are pretty much a badass.

"Commitment to self means that there is no hidden treasure or savior outside of ourselves. We are the ones we have been waiting for."
~ Heather Ash Amara

Suggested Practices to Cultivate and Connect to Your Inner Warrioress:

Take an assertive communication course and practice saying "no" more often to the demands on your time and energy. Keep healthy boundaries and create space between yourself and those you feel deplete your energy. Take a martial arts course or learn basic self-defense for women so that you know you can protect yourself if ever needed. Practice core exercises that strengthen your center, like Pilates, or practice several rounds every day of sun salutations from yoga. Practice sun salutations and the breath of fire every time you need to build up your strength and inner fire.

Watch the sunrise and feel the power of the sun entering your Solar Plexus, and as you do, set three clear intentions for the day with clarity and confidence asking yourself: "What do I want to create today?" Always have times of focused work followed by luscious play to make sure you don't burn out or get depleted. Practice affirmations and learn mindset training to redirect your thoughts when you start to tell yourself you can't do something, or you're not enough, or you're not strong or powerful. If ever you feel stuck in inaction, talk to your resistance inside like it's an old friend, and ask it why it's there... what does it need? Why have you needed it in the past? How has it kept you safe? What does this resistance need so it can feel safe and you can move forward into your dreams and desires effectively?

Get connected to your "why." In other words, what drives you? What motivates you deeply? What are you most passionate about and committed to in your life? And remind yourself of this every day to stay inspired and moving forward towards your dreams and goals. Let your most important goals and desires be your "north star" and stay focused on them every single day. Say no to any demands on your energy that are not aligned with your goals. Surround yourself with strong and powerful women who see you and believe in you every day, and who are not afraid of your power or their own (they are out there!).

"You carry both lightning and thunder in the space between your bones and your soul. Become the storm you are hiding from. A hurricane does not run from the rain."
~ Nikita Gill

Examples of the Warrioress Archetype:

In Mythology, Movies, and Stories:
Wonder Woman in new *Wonder Woman* movie (2017)
Trilogy in *The Matrix* movies (1999-
Athena: goddess of wisdom, craft, war, and justice in Greek mythology
Artemis: goddess of the hunt, the moon, and the protector of nature in Greek mythology
Bast: the goddess of warfare in Egyptian Mythology
Nike: the goddess of speed, strength, and victory in Greek Mythology
Durga: the warrior goddess and fierce protector mother goddess in Hindu mythology

Historical or Contemporary Examples:
Joan of Arc: war heroine of France in 15th century, canonized as a Roman Catholic saint.
Rosa Parks: activist in the Civil Rights movement
Amelia Earhart: American aviator and first woman to fly solo across the Atlantic Ocean
Malala Yousafzai: author, Pakistani activist for female education and the youngest-ever Nobel Prize laureate
Heatherash Amara: author of the Warrior Goddess Training series
Hillary Clinton: former Secretary of State, first woman to win the popular vote in a US presidential election
Sofiah Thom: creative muse, mentor, embodiment coach and dancer

Cynthia Kersey: Founder of the Unstoppable Foundation
Marie Forleo: author, speaker, online marketing guru
Novalena Nichele: author of *The Total Female Package*
Lisa Sasevich: the "Queen of Sales Conversions," author, leader,
expert online sales and marketing consultant

> I wish I could show you
> When you are lonely
> Or in the darkness
> The astonishing light
> Of your own being
> ~ Hafiz

Affirmations to Help Reclaim Your Inner Warrioress:
JUST DO IT.
I can. I will. I am. NOW.
I am an unstoppable force of Love.
I work passionately and ceaselessly for the Highest Good.
I turn my vision into action.
I am fiercely committed to that which I hold as sacred.
I confidently move forward in the direction of my dreams and let
nothing get in my way.
I am resilient, strong, and powerful.

Music to Invoke the Warrioress Archetype:
I Choose by India Arie
My Fight Song by Rachel Platten
You Are the Universe by the Brand New Heavies
This Girl Is On Fire by Alicia Keys
May I Be Strong by Sasha Butterfly
I Will Survive by Gloria Gaynor

Storytime ~ How I Reclaimed My Own Inner Warrioress:

When I was in my late twenties and living in Encinitas, CA, I was engaged to be married to the man I thought was my soul mate. We had a beautiful relationship, and it was the first true deep connection I had let myself feel in many many years. Before we got married, we found out we were pregnant, which for me was a miracle as I had been told many times that I would never be able to conceive and have children. Needless to say, I was ecstatic to find out we were pregnant. This was the first chosen pregnancy I had experienced after my abortions, and I felt blessed and excited to be welcoming this experience in a whole new way than I had in my teens.

About four months into the pregnancy, I had a miscarriage. It was dreadfully painful and incredibly traumatic. I lost massive amounts of blood and the painful laboring and contracting process went on for over two weeks. My doctor finally called me in to do a D&C procedure, which is basically a procedure like an abortion to clean out your womb from any remaining tissue so your body will stop laboring and contracting.

I was not only physically completely debilitated from the experience, I was emotionally a wreck. I had invested so much hope and joy into this pregnancy, and I genuinely wanted to be a mother with all my heart. I was truly heartbroken. My partner and my relationship took a very big hit from the loss. Not long after, we broke our engagement and went our separate ways. This completely leveled and devastated me. The combined losses were too much for me to handle all at once, especially with my body still recovering from the physical, hormonal changes of the pregnancy loss. I really wasn't sure if I wanted to go on any longer with my life, and I went into a deep and dark depression with anxiety so high I could barely function. I was hardly able to work, but had also run out of any savings or financial resources to take time off any longer. Something needed to change and fast, or I was going to find myself heartbroken AND broke.

And then something magical happened. I had been leading women's circles for a few years at the time, and was still dreaming of starting my own business running women's retreats and workshops full time. When I looked at my life around me and saw what had become of it, I knew there was only one place to go from where I was... and that was up. In the depths of my suffering and pain, I reconnected to my dreams and desires once again, and I felt a fire lit within me to finally make these dreams come true. It was either that or wither away, and I chose life.

But my Warrioress had to be ignited. I needed to dig down deep and take action and move forward quickly. I needed to cut through all my deep self-doubts and self-criticism that was triggered through the losses and to fight for what was most important to me with all my heart. I wanted to help other women heal, and finally make a living from sharing my gifts, but I had very little business skills or masculine drive to make it all happen up to that point. I started to seek out expert support and guidance, and made a plan for how I would do it on little to no financial foundation. I built a website (not so easy in that time) and made business cards.

I practiced yoga religiously and did sun salutations every day at sunrise facing the eastern sun over the mountains outside my window. I committed to a disciplined meditation and breathwork practice every day to center and realign my energy and stay on track. In a fairly short time of consistent, disciplined action, I pulled myself back together, became certified as a yoga teacher and Reiki healer, and developed a series of women's workshops and retreats based around the chakra system (much of that work I still share today here in this pathway).

I didn't know much about marketing or business, but I had developed a fierceness and a resilience after my recent losses that helped me get crystal clear on what I wanted to create with my life. So, I just kept putting one foot in front of the other and grew my little business from nothing into something that supported me to have a simple but happy lifestyle in one of the most beautiful places in the world, though I definitely had to ask for a lot of help to cultivate business skills that were not natural for me. After a year of leading workshops, teaching yoga, seeing private clients for yoga therapy and energy work and hosting retreats, I made enough money to get on my feet again. It was then that a bigger vision emerged for me. I decided I was finally ready to go back to Boston University and finish my degree at last.

I was able to reinstate my scholarship (which was a miracle at the time as it had been over eight years since I left school) and made a plan for how I was going to go back and get my BA, and then go on to get my Masters in Counseling Psychology and become a holistic oriented psychotherapist, coach and teacher. And I did just that. I became a manifesting maniac and just kept calling forth that inner resilience and strength that I had found in my darkness to make it all happen, one step in front of the other. I kept my north star in mind, and focused on every step I needed to take to get there.

To this day, I look back to those years as the precious time where I first found my powerful inner Warrioress. I was able to rise from the ashes after one of the most difficult experiences of my life through finding her within me and calling her forth to lead the way. I learned what I was made of and how I truly could do anything I desired if I aligned my mind, heart and action all as one. And I had to fight for all of it, but I fought from the deepest place of self - love and being connected to my purpose and calling. I was willing to do anything to bring my dreams forth from this place of authentic passion and will, and I still am now to this day.

Questions for Reflection:

What feelings or emotions are activated through exploring this archetype? When have you experienced your own inner Warrioress ignited in your life? Where do you need to call her forth more in your life to move your dreams and desires forward? What practices can you commit to this week to activate your Warrioress more?

The 3rd Chakra: Manipura or Solar Plexus
Color: Yellow
Element: Fire
Seed sound: Ram
Stones to Help Balance: Calcite, Citrine, Topaz, Tiger's Eye

The 3rd Chakra is located above the navel and in the digestive area at the Solar Plexus. It is the center of our inner power, confidence, self-esteem, and discernment. It is where we source our inner fire and our Warrioress energy when we need to power through with courage and resilience. When balanced, we feel healthy boundaries with the world and have inner courage and confidence. When out of balance, we feel like we don't know how to separate our energy from other people's energy, and our energy feels "blah," wishy-washy, and defeated. Or it may be on overdrive and depleted, unable to relax into our receptivity and softness.

Practice the mantras that go along with this chakra, and you are invited to surround yourself with shades of yellow and gold here to help activate and balance this chakra. Feel your solar plexus shining like a bright shining sun. If you're able, do 2-3 rounds of sun salutations to the music suggested for the Warrioress archetype, or practice the breath of fire before you need to exert energy to power through a situation (just search sun salutations and/or breath of fire on Youtube if you are not sure how to do them… there are thousands of videos to guide you through this yoga sequence and/or breathing exercise). This combination of exercises will get you in touch with your physical, mental, emotional, and spiritual strength all at once.

Solar Plexus Chakra Mantras:
I am powerful.
I am strong.
I shine like the sun.

"A strong woman is one who feels deeply
and loves fiercely.
Her tears flow as abundantly as her laughter.
A strong woman is both soft and powerful,
practical and spiritual.
A strong woman is in her essence
A gift to the world."

~ Native American Saying

Chapter 6

The Artist Archetype: Open Your Creative Heart

Heart Chakra

"Don't ask yourself what the world needs, ask yourself what makes you come alive. And then go and do that. Because what the world needs is more people who have come alive."
~ Harold Whitman

In the *Reclaim Your Power* journey, as I have said many times, we go back to our early experiences in order to become more aware of who we are in the world today. We reclaim what shaped us, and re-vision what we want to create that is most aligned with our gifts from our wholeness. Building on the foundation of the Warrioress, who represents the courage to put ourselves out there and manifest what we want in the world, we move into the Artist. She represents a connection to our creative endeavors, and our courage to put our work out there from our hearts. She in a way is a marriage of masculine energy and feminine energy within us by taking action to put our heart's desires and feminine life force energy and creativity into form. She ultimately represents feeling connected to our hearts, our creativity, and bringing the beauty of our emotional depth into form through our art, whatever art we may choose.

Who Is She?

The Artist archetype embodies freedom and creative self-expression. She is open to the flow of life moving through her and is able to utilize this life force energy for her own creative endeavors and visions, or for supporting those of others. She can transform her creative visions from the mental/spiritual/intangible form into the tangible form with beauty as her guide. She is colorful, energetic, magical, vibrant, fertile, flowing and full of LIFE. She has both the masculine and feminine energy required to create new art and bring it forth into the world. She expresses her HEART in her ART and creativity is an expression of love for her. She FEELS deeply and allows herself to go deep into grief and high into love… because both are a source of her magic and creativity. She lets herself feel all of life, not just the pretty stuff, but the agony and pain as well. Her creations come from the depth of her connection to life itself and being willing to let it all in and let it all out. Her art can become a way of healing herself (and the world), moving from pain and suffering into the alchemy of something beautiful and transformative. Her art is how she experiences freedom and how she is fully expressing her vibrancy and gifts in this world.

The Shadow Side:

When out of balance or not connected to her art, she feels shut down and feels she has no creative resources or new ideas. She may feel abandoned by God or by life and not sure what purpose she has if she is not connected to her art or her expressive gifts. She may not know what value she holds for others if she is not entertaining or expressing, and feel lost when she is not connected to her persona of the artist. She may not be able to be in the stillness and silence of the void in between her creative inspirations without going into depression or despair (and yet so often these times of darkness can then lead to her next creative inspiration as well). She can also be so lost in her creativity and visions that she has no ability to execute the ideas that come. Or she may have trouble balancing her creative skills with her practical business skills. She may be so in her creative flow that she forgets to care for her body properly and be on a creative "high" that depletes her body over time if she is not mindful of her energy. She may at times feel like a "starving artist," which buys into a cultural myth of devaluing creativity as something that will not bring abundance. She may buy into this if it is her own experience of struggle, as if it is something she can only do for fun and not to make a living.

Why Reclaim Her?

When the artist is not alive in us as women, there can be a feeling of rigidity, or being overly serious and controlling without knowing how to play. We may experience a rise in fertility issues, or physical blocks in our reproductive systems, or blocks in our heart energy of giving and receiving. We may feel trapped, stuck in our masculine energy of DOING and PRODUCING, rather than playing and being free. Many of us as women are now working careers that require us to be in more of our masculine energy, and this can disconnect us from this vital, feminine, creative juicy energy we need inside. If this is the case, we may feel starved for feminine flow and movement and burdened by rigidity and schedules, too much mind chatter, not enough body connection, and feel perpetually burned out. Life can seem more black and white than colorful. We may feel simply cut off from inspiration and creative new thoughts.

In order to reclaim her, we have to let ourselves be young at heart again, and create for the sake of creating itself, not just to produce a "product" but to feel alive. We have to find creative outlets that are serving for our Soul and playful. As we do this, we open our creativity in all areas of our lives: in business, family, and relationships of all kinds.

We can also reclaim the artist inside of us by opening our heart to all of life, receiving its beauty and its darkness. Sometimes when we tap into our greatest despair, we touch into our greatest source of energy and beauty. Some of the artists out there who have made the most famous and powerful love songs, paintings and poems have done so from touching deeply into their painful life experiences, as well as their joyful ones.

When we shut down to our emotions (no matter the type) we block our creative life force energy moving through us. It gets stuck in the heart or the body rather than moving through in the cathartic, transmuting way as art and creativity can invite. It's vital for women to be open to their true feelings, and allow them to move through us with respect and love. All our feelings deserve to be felt, and none of them are "bad" feelings or too much. We as women are feeling and sensitive creatures and feel a full range of life every day. We so often shut down what we feel because we are called "sensitive" or too soft. But this softness and sensitivity is a woman's (and artist's) greatest gift. Our sensitivity allows us to feel emotions and move them through our body, as well as have compassion and empathy for the suffering of others. Our sensitivity is actually our superpower, and our hearts are our greatest asset we have to fuel our mission and our lives with love.

When You Are Connected to Your Healthy Inner Artist:

You feel ALIVE, colorful, and expressed. You allow yourself to take in all of life, the darkness and the light, and you allow yourself to feel your emotions fully rather than stuff them down. You create from the depth of your emotions, because when you let yourself feel fully you then choose to move the energy in a cathartic and transformative way rather than stuffing them down. Whether it be you create poetry, paintings, jewelry, delicious meals, powerful experiences, beautiful relationships or healthy children, you create from feeling deeply and trusting your emotions, both joyful and painful ones. Your range of what you can create is limitless because when you are tapped into your artist, your creativity is available for all areas of life, not just traditional "art" itself. Your presence lights up others and inspires people to be more colorful and creative themselves. You are connected to your body and you listen to its needs for movement, rest, pleasure, beauty and stillness.

> *"Go and make interesting mistakes, make amazing mistakes, make glorious and fantastic mistakes. Break rules. Leave the world more interesting for your being here. Make. Good. Art."*
> ~Neil Gaiman

Suggested Practices to Cultivate and Connect to Your Inner Artist:

Move your body in whatever way makes you feel good and free; dance, be spontaneous, be fluid in your movement rather than rigid and structured. Breathe deeply and often. Take in the breath of life fully into your lungs and body and imagine it to be removing creative blocks within you. Turn on your favorite music and sing at the top of your lungs or write your own music. Get outside in nature and away from technology often to be inspired by pure, natural elements. Get out of your routine and play, be silly, be present. Get in touch with your heart and your emotions and let yourself feel them fully, then allow them to be expressed however you feel called: writing, dancing, talking, singing, screaming, sharing. Put yourself around water, whether a river, the ocean, a lake, pond, or take a bath or shower. Being around water helps to clear energetic blocks and open to your natural flow of creativity. Have a good cry. Get a bunch of crayons, markers, and pens and color freely or with a coloring book or mandala. Make a Creativity Vision Board by cutting out pictures you love or feel drawn to from a magazine, then reassemble them on a poster board however you want and allow it to be an expression of your creative vision for your life and dreams. Try abdominal massage, or belly dancing and moving your hips in circular movements to open your energetic creative centers. Surround yourself with colors you love, and consume or listen to art (of all kinds) that inspire you and put you in touch with your own heArt.

"We don't sing to sound good, we sing to be FREE."
~ Jess Magic

Examples of the Artist Archetype:

In Mythology and Stories:
Erzulie: Haitian African spirit of beauty, art, jewelry, dance, luxury, and flowers
Muses: goddess of music, art, and science from Greek Mythology
Benzaiten: Japanese Buddhist goddess of everything that flows: water, time, words, speech, eloquence, and music.
Saraswati: goddess of creativity, art, and music in Hindu mythology
Meret: goddess of singing, dancing, and rejoicing in Egyptian mythology

Historical or Contemporary Examples:
Frida Kahlo: Mexican self-portrait artist, feminist icon
Martha Graham: American dancer and choreographer
Georgia O'Keeffe: famous female American artist of the 20th
century
Elizabeth Gilbert: American author, essayist, short story writer,
biographer, novelist, and memoirist
Laura Hollick: Soul Art Shaman, creative spiritual entrepreneur,
lover of the Earth
Shiloh Sophia McCloud: artist, founder of Intentional Creativity
and Cosmic Cowgirls
Jess Magic: speaker, HeArtist, sacred activist, musician, founder of
Free your Voice

"The artist never entirely knows — We guess. We may be wrong,
but we take leap after leap in the dark"
~ Agnes de Mille

Affirmations to Help Reclaim Your Inner Artist:
I surrender to the infinite flow of life force energy moving through
me.
I allow free time for creative inspiration to move through me in
whatever way it desires.
I allow my heart to be opened and expressed through my art.
I trust in the full range of my emotions as all vital to my creativity.
I listen to and follow my desires for play, fun, and childlike
creativity.
I allow my body to move freely with grace, ease, surrender, and
passion.

Music to Invoke the Artist Archetype:
All music! All music is a form of art, and all music can evoke different emotions for different people to help put you in touch with your inner artist and creativity. Find music that helps you feel your feelings, and play with the full range of emotions that music can evoke to support you in fueling your own creativity.

Other suggestions:
Forgiveness by India Arie
The Be Love Song by Alysse Fischer
Heart Sutra by Wah!
The Lover Inside of Me by Jess Magic
Give Love by MC Yogi

Storytime ~ How I Reclaimed My Own Inner Artist:

Let's revisit my mid-twenties again to recall how my inner Artist came to have a place in my life. I was living in Encinitas and had been wanting to find a creative outlet, but always felt like I was not a very creative person. I had a story that because I had never learned to paint, sing, draw, or dance choreographed dances, I was not artistic. I also had struggled with fertility issues for many years, so this just fueled my story inside that there was something inherently wrong with my ability to create, whether it was art or children or anything well for that matter.

But I REALLY loved jewelry and stones. I had always had many pieces in my own collection, and loved having healing rocks and gemstones from the earth all around me. I had collected stones from the time I was a little girl everywhere I went, and I loved the fact that jewelry was a combination of style, adornment, healing stones, and art all in one. However, I didn't think I could actually recreate the things I loved to wear.

But I tried anyway. As I have shared here already, my twenties were a time of a lot of healing and self-discovery for me. I found my passions and my gifts throughout these years in a profound way. When I discovered making jewelry, it opened up a creative outlet where I got to play and explore and turn ideas from my head into form with my hands. I made pieces that symbolized certain concepts or healing intentions for women, and I eventually had a small jewelry business that brought in a nice little income.

Once, on a full moon night after a particularly hard week, I had a vision come to me for a necklace that felt like it was truly from the Goddess herself. I went to my jewelry table and trusted my inner guidance to create this piece from an abalone spiral shell and green peridot stones. When I finished, I was absolutely in love and didn't think I would ever take it off. It was my first time creating something where it did not feel like I had made it myself, but rather that I was a vessel for it to come through me. I named this piece "the Sacred Spiral." It became for me a symbol of my own sacred feminine healing journey, and I wanted to wear it as a reminder every day.

In trusting this creative vision to come through me, I had many abundant blessings unfold as a result. I sold necklace after necklace off my body to women I met on the street, and in street fairs, and even was asked to put them into Whole Foods Markets. This was a time I was wanting very much to transition out of my nutritional therapy caregiving job and move towards working with women and doing healing work. This necklace literally funded that transition for me to do so until my new business took off.

My inner Artist tapped into my creative desire and intention to be a healing force for women. She found a way to express her creativity that was fitting and perfect for me. I learned to trust my creative visions and allow them to be birthed rather than judge myself for not being artistic enough. To this day, I am very connected to my inner Artist and love this part of myself. I find now that she has many expressions and outlets, from dancing, to painting, to graphic design, to cooking, to poetry, to writing, to coloring with my daughter... and more.

That period of birthing the Sacred Spiral necklace was the first time I learned to trust and empower her to be expressed fully in my life. Now if I go too long without being creative in some way, I feel flat and dull. I honor my creativity as unique to me, and do my best not to compare myself or judge my expressions against those of others. This is also another reason the spiral has become such a common symbol in all my work. It reminds me of this powerful and precious time where I learned to trust my own visions and creativity once again.

Questions for Reflection:

What feelings or emotions are activated within you through exploring this archetype? How is your own inner Artist being expressed right now in your life? How do you desire for her to be expressed? What are some practices you can commit to this week to invite your inner Artist to come out and play?

The 4th Chakra: Anahata - The Heart
Color: Green (or also Light Pink)
Element: Air
Seed Sound: Yam
Stones to Help Balance: Peridot, Green Tourmaline,
Jade, Rose Quartz

The heart chakra is found right at the center of the chest, and represents our emotional center of compassion, forgiveness, kindness, and love. When the heart feels blocked, it can be difficult to open up or feel connected to life, to our mission, and to our relationships. We may feel we want to hide in order to protect ourselves from being hurt. When open, we feel space for all of our emotions, and are kind with ourselves when we don't feel the happier ones. We allow ourselves to be vulnerable and honest with ourselves and others and to share our love openly without hoarding or holding it back. We have deep self-love and self-compassion, and that translates into an authentic love for others.

Practice the mantras here, and you are invited to surround yourself with or wear shades of green (or light pink) if you'd like to help activate the heart chakra as well. Go to Youtube and choose any of the "heart chakra music" or "heart chakra chants" that appeal to you, or choose any music that feeds your artist soul! Allow yourself to simply be with any feelings or emotions that arise, and practice trusting (especially when it's hard) that your heart has the space to feel it all with love and compassion.

Heart Chakra Mantras:
I have space to feel it all.
I am compassionate.
I am Love.

"We dance for laughter, we dance for tears, we dance for madness, we dance for fears, we dance for hopes, we dance for screams, we are the dancers, we create the dreams."
~ Albert Einstein

Chapter 7

The Queen Archetype: Treat Yourself Royally, Speak Your Truth

Throat Chakra

"In every woman there is a Queen. Speak to the Queen, and the Queen will answer."
~ Norwegian Proverb

Next, we move deeper into the energy of our self-expression, and look at how we ask for our needs to be met from a place of power within us. Building on the foundation we have created so far, the Queen can be called forth to support the actions necessary to speak up for yourself and ensure you are taking the very best care of yourself possible. She taps into your power and confidence from self-love, and moves from that place in the world. She ensures that you are living in alignment with your inner truth, and has the courage to speak up and course corrects when not. For many young women, we were not taught this level of self-care and courage, and the Queen is an opportunity to reclaim your voice and confidence so you can step fully into the empowered woman you know you want to be in the world.

Who Is She?

She carries herself regally, and treats herself with consistent love and respect. She speaks her needs with confidence and self-assurance. She has a noble and regal quality about her, and her beauty shines from the inside out because she takes loving care of herself. She attracts support with grace and ease because she knows her needs are sacred, and she makes sure they are met. The people around her want to serve her because they trust her judgment and integrity. She knows her inherent value and does not let people treat her with disrespect. If they do, they will not remain in her life for long.

She speaks her truth, has the hard conversations, and is willing to say the things that others are not. She knows that in doing so, she is serving the highest good of all. She delegates masterfully and asks for help regularly. She gets more done by doing less. She maintains peace within herself because she is regularly communicating her thoughts, feelings, and needs, rather than suppressing them inside. She leads from her heart, and others want to follow her because of her kindness and benevolence.

She is powerful and strong and also fiercely loving. She is sometimes feared for her fierceness, but, ultimately, she is respected and admired for her consistent truth telling, authenticity and vulnerability. She stands in the truth of her wise inner knowing of what is right and good and acts on it. In general, she doesn't put up with any B.S.

The Shadow Side:

When the Queen energy is out of balance or not nurtured within, she may feel unworthy of being served or supported by others. She doesn't see how beautiful and powerful she is, and doesn't feel deserving of regal treatment. She may spend all her time serving others, but inside be filled with resentment and anger because she is constantly feeling like her needs are not being met. This may lead to her always feeling like a victim. She blames others for not meeting her needs, and does not know how to decipher what is hers to do and what is others' to do.

She may also blame others for not meeting her needs when often she is actually angry at herself for not knowing how to ask that they be met effectively, or not knowing how to meet them from within her own resources. She is regularly overwhelmed trying to "do it all" and feels she can't get a moment in for herself. When she does take care of herself, she may feel guilty or like it's too much of a luxury, rather than it being totally necessary and important to her life as a woman. The other extreme if the queen is in overdrive, she may be so demanding on others that she expects them to serve her all the time in an unrealistic way, which is the tyrant or dictator energy instead, and does not take into account the well-being of those around her.

Why Reclaim Her?

As women, we all need to come home to our own power and grace inside, and find our own authentic version of our Queen within us. The Queen inside us is the one who speaks her truth. She is our confidence, our assertiveness, and our knowing that we deserve to be treated royally (yes, we ALL do). Depending on how we are raised or what culture we are brought up in, many of us as women are taught that it's not OK to ask for our needs to be met, or we are taught that a woman is meant to primarily serve the needs of others. We may think she is not allowed to be demanding because being a wife, mother or a woman means mostly self-sacrifice. This is an old paradigm and could not be further than the truth. This belief has kept us in a state of disempowerment and exhaustion for centuries.

We are in a time where women's empowerment is rising all over the planet (though we still have a lot of work to do) and we are starting to finally wake up to the inherent truth of our equality with men – that we are equally deserving of all rights that men enjoy. Though the women's rights movement has been in motion for many years, we are starting to actually see and know that we can do anything we desire. We are seeing it manifested in the world around us as women are almost getting elected as President of the United States, and more and more women entrepreneurs are rocking it in business. But we need strength, energy and abundance to really be at our fullest capacity, in whatever role we play as women.

We are collectively starting to know the power of our incredible feminine gifts and are having the confidence to share them with the world more and more. And it takes a tremendous amount of self-care to keep our wells full so we can be at our best for the world, for our families, for our commitments... and not burn out completely.

Unfortunately, in generations past (and still in many cultures and countries today), it was not safe to speak your truth as a woman and have a voice. It was not safe to be strong, or you may be punished or even killed in extreme situations. But now (at least in our culture) we are starting to use our voice. We as women are waking up and rising into our power, becoming more assertive, self-expressed and honest so we can become the Queens we have always been destined to be. Though this is still something we are learning collectively and stepping into together, it is becoming more and more prevalent. But that doesn't necessarily make it any easier!

Women deserve to be treated royally, but we must first know that about ourselves and treat ourselves with love and respect above all. We must make the choices to remove ourselves from relationships and situations where we are not treated with respect. We have to become the protectors of our own hearts and know that we deserve the absolute best. A Queen does not tolerate disrespect. Sadly, so many women still struggle in abusive or challenging relationships they feel deep down they deserve.

We so often see Queen figures depicted negatively in fairy tales or movies. We don't have a lot of healthy examples of Queens in our lives and the world. But we are all Queens deserving of love and respect, therefore we have a responsibility to ourselves and the world around us to proclaim our needs and make sure they are met so we can be at our best. We also have to be able to hold the space for the people in our lives to ask for the same and be willing to meet the needs of others with the same type of honor as we expect them to meet ours.

No matter where you have been or what has happened in your life, it is time for all of us to reclaim our inner Queens...once and for all.

When You Are Connected to Your Healthy Inner Queen:

You feel rested, at peace, and supported because you know you are not alone in the efforts of your life. You are surrounded with people who love and respect you, because you have taught the world how you want and deserve to be treated. You have created a support system of help around you that is happy to show up for you and meet your needs. People like to serve you, because they are rewarded with love and kindness. They know they can depend on you as well when they need your support. You are not afraid to make mistakes and take chances, because you know you can always make things right and start over again if needed. You communicate your love in many ways to those around you and do not hold back from expressing your gratitude, affection and appreciation of others. You demand (with love) that your environment and those in it be supportive, positive and uplifting. Your space and home is treated like a sanctuary and you take care to maintain healthy energy within it every day.

You are not afraid to ask for what you need from the world; you are willing to do it even when it's not comfortable. You have had enough experience in doing this to know that when you get to the other side of a hard conversation, you always feel more free and better inside (even when the other person is not able to fully receive your words). You are free from blocked or stuck emotions inside because you take regular care to keep your heart and mind clear and open. You take royal care of yourself. Even after times of hard work, you know you will take the time to balance it with pleasure, joy, fun and rest. You carry yourself with confidence, and are not quick to blow up on others because you have created peace and spaciousness inside you that is lasting and real. You empower the Queen in other women. You do not compete with them or take part in catty gossip that belittles other women because you have confidence in yourself and your own gifts. You honor the women in your life with the respect they deserve, and in doing so, you help uplift all women in the world.

"Think like a Queen. A Queen is not afraid to fail.
Failure is another stepping stone to greatness."
~ Oprah Winfrey

Suggested Practices to Cultivate and Connect to Your Inner Queen:

Practice speaking your truth regularly, especially when it feels most vulnerable. Make sure you get out your feelings respectfully when they arise. Take a realistic assessment of your life and see if your needs for rest, sleep, exercise, creativity, pampering, fun, friendship… and whatever else you desire, are honestly being adequately met. If you feel regularly depleted, depressed, or exhausted, likely they are not. Get real with what you need to thrive, and commit to taking care of yourself royally (at least once) every day, even in the midst of busy lives and demands on your energy. Take baths, use essential oils you love on your skin and in your home, get manicures and pedicures (if that's your thing), and indulge in massages. These treatments may seem like a luxury (and sometimes they are!) but they can become much more of a regular part of our lives if we really see the importance of maintaining pleasure, fun and pampering to stay balanced. We begin to see how this contributes to our mental health and well-being, and how this makes us better for all those around us. Create a "Queen's Day" retreat for yourself where you do only things that feel nourishing and totally pampering for yourself. To really step into your Queen… ask for support to make it happen from your friends and family around you!

"Every woman is a queen, and we all have different things to offer."
~ Queen Latifah

Examples of the Queen Archetype:

In Mythology, Movies, and Stories:
Snow White: in *Snow White and the Huntsman* (2012)
Mab: Queen of the Fairies in English Folklore
Guinevere: in Arthurian legend, the wife and Queen to King Arthur
Anatu: Mesopotamian goddess, ruler of the earth and queen of the sky
Marisha-Ten: in Japanese mythology, queen of heaven, goddess of light, of sun and moon

Historical or Contemporary Examples:
Cleopatra: born 69 BC, the last active ruler of Ptolemaic Egypt
Queen Nandi of the Zulu Kingdom: mother of Shaka Zulu
Grace Kelly: American actress who became Princess of Monaco
Audrey Hepburn: British actress, dancer, model, humanitarian
Maya Angelou: American poet, memoirist, and civil rights activist
Meryl Streep: Academy Award winning actress and philanthropist
Michelle Obama: activist, lawyer, first African American First Lady of the United States
Oprah: American media proprietor, talk show host, actress, producer, and philanthropist
Debbie Lichter: congruency mentor and food addiction expert
Gayle Larson: author, public speaking coach and mentor, founder of Real Speaking

> *"She's the kind of queen that knows her crown isn't on her head, but in her Soul."*
> ~ Adrian Michael

Affirmations to Help Reclaim Your Inner Queen:
I ask for what I need with confidence and grace.
I assert my power with love.
I trust that what makes me feel whole is for the highest good of all.
I trust I will always know how to meet my needs from self-care and love.
When I experience wholeness, my heart can give from a place of fullness.
I treat myself royally… because I am a Queen.
I share my story with the world with confidence and grace.

Music to Invoke the Queen Archetype:
Video (Because I am a Queen) by India Arie
Brave by Sara Bareilles
Roar by Katy Perry
Express Yourself by Madonna
Confident by Demi Lovato
Everybody Got Their Something by Nikka Costa
Respect by Aretha Franklin

Storytime ~ How I Reclaimed My Own Inner Queen:
I have come to realize the power of my inner Queen most profoundly in my relationship with my husband, Jonathan. My husband and I were friends for many months before we started dating, as both of us were in long term committed relationships prior to coming together. We started dating very soon after I broke up with my previous boyfriend. At the time, I had convinced myself I wasn't looking for anything serious and actually wanted some time off of dating after a two-year relationship.

Jonathan was in the same place. After coming out of his previous relationship, he had convinced himself that he needed to "play the field" a bit and not get too serious about anyone. He had just moved into a total bachelor pad with two of his best entrepreneur bachelor friends. All three vowed to have a year of fun with no serious girlfriends. Jonathan had only had serious girlfriends for his entire adult life, one long term relationship after another, so this was something new and different he thought he needed to experience before settling down with "the one."

But quite unexpectedly, we had a powerful, beautiful connection from day one once we started dating. We went very deep very fast. Both of us were somewhat afraid to admit this because the intensity of what we felt was so beautiful, but also scary. I had thought when we first started dating that I didn't want anything serious, and that I was OK to just "hang out" and not get too involved. But as time went on, my feelings for him became very strong. I started to foresee a future with him I did not expect. I realized that it was not my truth anymore to be casually dating. It wasn't actually the truth of what we were experiencing in our connection together either.

Jonathan, remembering his original intention of the single man bachelor pad, came to me and asked me what I would think if he said, hypothetically speaking, that he wanted to date several women at once and not be exclusive. This was just at the time we started getting very close and much more intense in our connection, so it was an interesting experience for me. I sat with it, and prayed on it, and let myself release any anger or frustration about it being "wrong." Then I tuned in inside myself. I felt into what was best and most honoring of my heart. I was totally honest with myself about what I truly wanted and needed.

I came to a place of total peace and freedom inside around it all. Even though I had strong feelings for him, I completely surrendered and let it go, trusting that the relationship that was right for me would come at the right time, and I would never have to settle for anything less than what I wanted and deserved.

I came back to him and said, "That sounds wonderful if that's what you want, but it's not what I'm looking for right now. I thought it was, and now I feel differently, so I give you my total blessing to do whatever you need to do right now for yourself. I have loved getting to know you and spending time with you, and I will forever be grateful for this time together. But casually dating is not for me right now and I'm ready to call in the true long-term relationship I envision for myself."

I genuinely felt it as I said this to him. I delivered it with self-love, confidence, and grace. I loved him deeply already, and yet I let him go in that moment with total trust and respect for myself. And within two or three days of this conversation, Jonathan came back and was spilling his heart out to me and professing how much he loved me and wanted to be with me. It was a very fast turnaround. He had also thought he wanted something else, but with me standing in my truth and being totally confident in my worth and my needs, it made him realize what he really wanted, too. He didn't want to not be with me for the sake of some lifestyle he thought he "should" experience. That wasn't actually his truth either. As I stood in my Queen and made sure I did not compromise my value and my needs, it called him into his King so he could meet me and be by my side. The truth is, he knew I would accept nothing less.

Within one month I was living with Jonathan in this bachelor pad (which was a very interesting experience in and of itself) and the playboy mansion dream never manifested for him. But it was by his choice, not because I forced it or manipulated him in any way. We both decided to dive in and fell hard and fast in love with each other. I became pregnant with our first child a little over a year later, and got married not long after that.

I have since that time had many opportunities to stand in my truth and use my voice to ask for what I need… from needing him help more with childcare, to needing more support in my business and dreams, to needing him to clean the house more (to name just a few areas). He has a very strong, intense, and at times somewhat wild personality that wants to be free to work like an entrepreneur on crack with no limitations. He needed a very strong woman to hold her ground by his side and call forth a more grounded version of himself. And because of this, I have had to learn to embrace my inner Queen and ask for my authentic needs to be met time and time again in our relationship. It has not been easy, but ultimately has been an incredible blessing for both of us.

I have learned to have the hard conversations with him that feel incredibly vulnerable and to stand in total respect and love for myself in the process. Speaking my truth and asking for what I need, though it is sometimes met with resistance at first (ok, let's be honest here...it's more like breaking a wild stallion at times), has time and time again called him into the King that he wants to be for me. This has made him into a better man because of it. My husband is the most devoted, loving, loyal, sensitive man I could ever have the blessing to love. I am so incredibly grateful for him and his continuous commitment to love and cherish me the best way possible in this lifetime.

I don't do it perfectly, that's for sure, but I do my best to truly assess my needs, be fair and just to what he needs too, and come from self-love, compromise, and honesty, not manipulation. And when we do this as women, we help elevate all those around us to a higher place. I could have easily compromised my truth many times along the way in our relationship. But because I didn't and still don't, I have continued to call forth the true commitment and love that I deserve, that we both deserve, and that we have both always wanted deep inside.

Questions for Reflection:

What feelings or emotions are activated within you through exploring this archetype? Where in your life do you need to call forth your Queen to have a voice and express her truth more? Imagine yourself having a hard conversation this week, but envision yourself feeling confident, radiant, and at peace as you do it. What is one practice you can commit to this week to help activate your inner Queen and give her permission to come forth in your life?

The 5th Chakra: Vishuddha - The Throat
Color: Light Blue or Turquoise
Element: Space
Seed Sound: Ham
Stones to Help Balance: Turquoise, Aqua Marine, Blue Calcite

The throat chakra is the center of communication and self-expression, and encompasses the throat, neck, mouth, and jaw areas. The throat chakra is the voice of the body. It is a pressure valve that allows the energy from the other chakras to be expressed. If it is out of balance or blocked it can affect the health of our whole system and we may literally even feel a lump in our throat when we try to communicate or cry. When in balance and open, we feel at peace, self-expressed, and free. We feel connected to our emotions and able to release them through some expressive medium, either talking singing, dancing, or art.

To help balance this chakra, try singing or chanting more often. You can choose either to one of these fun and empowering songs suggested here in the Queen archetype, or any song that makes you feel empowered as you sing it out loud. You are invited to wear or surround yourself with the colors of light blue and turquoise, and allow yourself time and space to use your voice often. Speak out any of the affirmations or mantras suggested here that feel good to you to empower your voice, or create your own. Perhaps incorporate these practices into a "Queen's Day Retreat" you create for yourself. Have a day where you pamper yourself with the things that make you feel nourished and treated royally.

Throat Chakra Mantras:

I am expressed and at peace.
I use my voice with confidence and love.
I speak my Truth.

"Our deepest fear is not that we are inadequate. Our deepest fear is that we are powerful beyond measure. It is our light, not our darkness that most frightens us. We ask ourselves, Who am I to be brilliant, gorgeous, talented, fabulous? Actually, who are you not to be? You are a child of God. Your playing small does not serve the world. There is nothing enlightened about shrinking so that other people won't feel insecure around you. We are all meant to shine, as children do. We were born to make manifest the glory of God that is within us. It's not just in some of us; it's in everyone. And as we let our own light shine, we unconsciously give other people permission to do the same. As we are liberated from our own fear, our presence automatically liberates others."

~ Marianne Williamson

Chapter 8

The Wise Woman Archetype: Trust Your Inner Wisdom

Third Eye Chakra

"You've always had the power within you, my dear.
You just had to learn it for yourself."
~ Glenda, the Good Witch in *The Wizard of Oz*

We have now arrived at the Wise Woman archetype. We are moving into a wise, ancient archetype that helps us connect us to a very deep place inside of us as women. The Wise Woman within us is the embodiment of our intuition and inner guidance system. So many of us as women either never felt connected to her, or did as children and then lost it over time. In reclaiming our power, we reclaim a wisdom inside of us that is independent of the outside world. We reclaim our inner voice of truth that is unshakable and real. We all have this Wise Woman inside, and we can trust that we know what is best and right for ourselves. We just have to get to know her, this still and calm voice inside, and allow her to have more say in our lives. When we listen to our inner Wise Woman, and trust the wisdom of our Soul, we can create a life aligned with our deep inner knowing rather than living one that is dictated by what the outside world wants from us.

Who Is She?

Our inner Wise Woman embodies deep feminine presence and ancient wisdom. She makes her choices from her own intuitions and inner knowing. She trusts the ancient knowing within her and knows her own life experience is sacred and trustworthy. She values it over the outside world's advice. She does not need to source her guidance from others because she knows what she knows inside and does not doubt and question it constantly. She knows her purpose in the cycle of life and takes a stand to protect life on earth for the next several generations to come. She draws upon her ancestor's' wisdom and the energy of the earth for guidance. No matter her age, she exudes maturity of years and wisdom. She is deeply connected to her inner Truth and speaks it without hesitation or fear. This is the part of ourselves that has lived many years and known many experiences, perhaps even your elderly self many years into the future who has really come to know herself and her values. She feels an authentic peace within because she knows what really matters in life and doesn't sweat the small stuff that one day will be forgotten. This deep, mysterious feminine wisdom may threaten others in the world because she is so tapped into Truth itself and does not waver in her certainty of what she knows deep inside.

The Shadow Side:

In her shadow, she can be depicted as the dark witch or old hag, or reclusive and disconnected from humanity. She can be resentful, senile and foolish if she is too connected to her inner world with no grounding here in the earthly realm or with real people in her life. A shadow part of the wise woman emerges if she feels disowned and disrespected, devalued and not listened to despite her wisdom. This is the part inside of us that we ignore despite her constant "nagging" on us of the truth. Our inner wise woman may become pissed off, bitter and resentful if she is treated as irrelevant and irrational. Just as the elderly sometimes feel disowned and disrespected because of their age, so does this wise part within ourselves feel ignored and dishonored every time we choose not to listen to our inner truth.

Why Reclaim Her?

Many of us as women were never taught how to listen to our own inner wisdom. In fact, unfortunately, we usually learned to do the opposite. We live in a culture that primarily values finding the answers outside of ourselves rather than looking within, and this has caused us to mistrust our own knowing overall. We have Google at our disposal to look up anything we want at any time, and we are surrounded with stimulation that pulls us in a thousand different directions every day. Taking time to get still, get quiet and go within to listen to our inner world is something that is not as encouraged in our pop culture. It is something that we have to come to value ourselves and take it upon ourselves to discover how to do.

And especially for women, who are such naturally intuitive, wise creatures, many of us have become disconnected from our own inner knowing and have replaced it with always seeking answers and wisdom from outside ourselves. We all naturally have intuition and even psychic abilities inside, because biologically we HAVE to in order to be able to intuitively mother young babies and understand their needs without them being able to communicate with us verbally. Whether we have children or not, we are biologically wired to be able to hear the unspoken, to see the unseen, and to know what is going on in any given situation by trusting our bodies' cues and intuitive hits.

When we are connected to our intuition, we are connected to our inner power. We are not as likely to follow the guidance of someone else who doesn't have our best interest in mind. We will likely make choices aligned with our highest good on a regular basis. If we do make mistakes, we will learn how to choose differently next time. Without being connected to our intuition and our inherent intuitive abilities, we are at the whim of outer influence and energies constantly. This can be very confusing and maddening for a woman.

We must as women learn to trust ourselves and reclaim our inner Wise Woman... to put her back in the driver's seat of our lives and trust in her more. She will never guide us wrong, if we really take the time to listen to her, even though sometimes her guidance scares us or forces us to make changes we are afraid to make (or simply don't want to make). We will live much more empowered, aligned lives with clarity, peace, and trust when we live from this place inside of us and regularly check in with her to make sure we are living in accordance with our highest path.

When You Are Connected to Your Healthy Inner Wise Woman:
You trust yourself to make good choices, because you know you will always have an inner guidance system to point you in the right direction. You feel confident in the direction you choose in life, because you have taken the time to get real and listen to what is truly aligned and right for you. You look for the wisdom that can be mined from the mistakes, and you are not hard on yourself when they happen. You pay attention to your dreams and honor their messages. You look for the signs and guideposts that come in all forms... and you don't write any "coincidence" off as insignificant or irrelevant. You are willing to look for guidance from those who are wise and have had much more experience than you, like your elders or the spirits of your ancestors. If they are truly good counsel for you, they will likely ask you questions that direct you back to your own intuition, rather than tell you what you should or should not do. You feel a maturity that is

independent of your age, and you can tune into what you would tell yourself twenty, thirty, forty years from now in your wise elder years. You know what's really important in life, and live each day as if it could be your last, not from a morbid place, but from a place of gratitude and appreciation for every day you are alive. You know that every day is a gift, and you want to cherish all your days on this beautiful earth.

> *"Don't let the noise of others' opinions drown out your own inner voice."*
> ~ Steve Jobs

Suggested Practices to Cultivate and Connect to Your Inner Wise Woman:

Practice being in a state of receptivity, slowing down and being still. We are usually in a state of movement, busyness, and doing, and don't take the time to be still and listen to our inner world. Meditation is one of the best ways to practice being in a state of receptivity and listening. Find a form that works for you and practice it regularly. Listen to your body. When you have a "gut" feeling, or you tense up suddenly, or a headache comes on in a certain situation or around certain people, get curious and listen to the messages of what your body may be saying to you. You can ask your body questions and then listen to what you receive. Your inner wisdom is found very much in your body's messages and signals. Some women feel their intuition in their wombs, some in their gut, some in their hearts. Pay attention to where you "feel" yours in your own body.

Practice free writing and journaling. Ask a question you are not sure about, and then allow your hand to write down freely whatever comes to you, with no agenda. Simply free write and allow whatever wants to come through you to be put down on paper. You may find that your intuition comes through in writing easier than in meditation or stillness. Pay attention to your dreams and regularly write them down. Ask the different figures or characters in your dreams what they are here to teach you, and journal about what you feel and experience in your dreams. Dreams can hold rich symbolic wisdom from our inner world as well as keys to unlocking deeper understanding about ourselves and our lives.

Pay attention to all the ways your intuition and inner wisdom speak to you. It may be through feelings, dreams, sounds, words, memories, writing, thoughts, psychic abilities, or a combination of these. Your task is to get to know your own inner Wise Woman, and figure out how YOU hear your own deepest wisdom.

"There is a voice that doesn't use words. Listen."
~ Rumi

Examples of the Wise Woman Archetype:

In Mythology, Movies, and Stories:
The Oracle Woman in *The Matrix* (1999)
Grandmother in *Moana* (2016)
Sophia: Wisdom Incarnate, the goddess of all those who are wise in Greek mythology
Athena: in Greek mythology, goddess of wisdom and military victory
White Buffalo Calf Woman: a sacred mythical figure of the Lakota people who is their primary cultural prophet

Historical or Contemporary Examples:
Gloria Steinem: feminist, writer, speaker
Alice Walker: American writer, poet, and activist
International Council of 13 Grandmothers: a diverse group of elders who devote their lives to prayer and action to help shift the direction of humanity
Clarissa Pinkola Estés PhD: American poet, Jungian psychoanalyst, author, spoken word artist
Dr. Anita Johnston, PhD: psychologist, author, speaker
Laura Lynne Jackson: psychic intuitive, certified medium, New York Times best-selling author
Judith Duerk: author of *Circle of Stones: Woman's Journey to Herself*
Renee Airya: author of *Flip your Flaws*, speaker, artist

"The most confused we ever get is when our heads try to convince our hearts of something we know is a lie."
~ Karen Moning

Affirmations to Help Reclaim Your Inner Wise Woman:
I can trust my inner voice to guide me and direct me.
I am deeply connected to my intuition and inner wisdom.
I am wise, and I know what I know.
I have a wise healing voice inside me that leads me to my highest good.
I pay attention to my body's wisdom and listen to its cues.
I am connected to the ancient wisdom of my ancestors inside me.
I listen to the Earth and Mother Nature's wisdom.

Music to Invoke the Wise Woman Archetype:
Om Mani Padme Hum by Wah!
May I Suggest by Red Molly
New Way by Imani and Friends
The Healing Room by Sinead O'Connor
Calling Wisdom by Karunesh

Storytime ~ How I Reclaimed My Own Inner Wise Woman:

My journey of reclaiming my intuition and trusting my inner wisdom has been a long road, with new layers of trust in myself emerging each step of the way. However, a time where I had a profound shift in trusting my intuition and inner guidance goes back to my time at Boston University again. In the Lover Archetype, I shared my story of leaving BU and going to Hawaii, however I did not share how that choice happened.

It was a cold winter night in Boston and I had come back from yet another long, grueling seven- to eight-mile run around the Charles River. I was lying on the floor in my dorm room, very thin and likely very hungry (by my own forced choice on myself), and felt totally exhausted and worn down to the bone. I remember thinking as I laid there that I didn't know how I was going to go on any longer like this. I had pushed myself to my limits, and nothing was working. On the outside, everything seemed great: a huge academic scholarship to BU, good jobs, straight A's, lots of friends... but I was miserable inside because I was not living my authentic dreams, and I was holding onto deep pain inside my heart from my past.

In that moment, I looked up at my wall where I had a poster of Hawaiian Spinner Dolphins on the wall. They were all smiling big happy grins and swimming freely in the turquoise blue Hawaiian waters. I saw a twinkle in their eyes that made me light up inside. I got up to look in the mirror and realized that I had lost the twinkle in my own eyes and I didn't know how to get it back. In that moment, I knew I needed help and that it was beyond my control. So, I asked God for guidance on what to do.

As soon as I asked this question, I truly felt as if a voice inside me yelled loudly, "Leave school and go to Hawaii to swim with those dolphins." And instantly I contracted, thinking to myself... "That is absolutely the craziest idea I have ever had, and it will NEVER happen." And yet it persisted. I heard the voice inside again, and though I was scared to death, I could not shake the prompting that was coming from a very deep place inside. Again,

I heard it, "Leave school and go to Hawaii to swim with those dolphins."

I could not believe this idea was coming to me. I was at a prominent university doing very well in a competitive academic program, on an almost full-ride scholarship. I was halfway through my junior year. I was almost done! How could I leave right then? What would my parents think? What would everyone think? How could I live with myself if I left it all and followed some CRAZY pull inside. I tried to shut the idea down, but something inside me couldn't shake it. The next day I went to the computer and saw there were discounted airline tickets to the Big Island of Hawaii from California for less than $200. Mind you I was in Boston, but hey... what's a short drive across the country to catch a flight, right?

I did the craziest thing I had ever done in my life. I purchased my ticket right then and there. A one-way ticket, and no plan for how I was going to make it all work. I had $500 to my name and a long journey ahead of me in order to get to those islands. But something in me just knew I had to do it. I felt this prompting in my body, like a pull to my Soul, not my head. In some way, I knew that my life and my health depended on it. So, against all the strong advice and naysayers, I chose to trust that calling. It turned out to be the best decision I had ever made in my life.

I finished out my semester at BU and took a leave of absence (a very long one). I share about my time out in Hawaii in a few stories here in this book so you know much more fully why that choice was so important for me. I landed there with absolutely nothing but a duffle bag, a couple of friends I knew on the island, and $250 to my name. Somehow, I was magically embraced by the islands and supported in every way I needed, one thing after the other.

I received a place to live, jobs, access to fresh fruit and vegetables on a farm, a free car to drive while I was there, and so, so much healing and transformation. It was exactly what I needed. I was held and nurtured back to life from a very dark place once again. I would never have experienced that if I didn't trust this crazy calling inside me – my inner Wise Woman and intuition guiding me to exactly where I needed to go, despite ALL the logical reasons why I shouldn't do it.

I did return to BU many years later, in my own time and when I was ready to complete my degree. I graduated Magna Cum Laude with Honors, and I went on to get my Master's Degree at Pacifica Graduate Institute after that. I followed my inner Wise Woman and intuition in that decision as well. It turned out to be another one of the best decisions I had ever made. I have come to learn over time that I can always trust that part of myself, but I have to call her forth and give her the driver's seat in my life. This is not easy, and takes such diligence and practice every day on my part.

But even when she invites me to take a huge leap of faith and make difficult choices and changes, she ultimately has never led me in the wrong direction.

Questions for Reflection:

What feelings or emotions are activated through exploring this archetype? Where have you listened to your Wise Woman before and had a positive outcome? When have you ignored her and had a difficult experience? What is one message NOW you can feel coming from your inner Wise Woman? What the practices you are willing to commit to this week to help cultivate your inner Wise Woman and listen to her more?

The 6th Chakra: Ajna or 3rd Eye
Color: Indigo Blue or Violet Purple
Element: Mind
Seed Sound: Om
Stones to Help Balance: Amethyst, Lapis Lazuli

Ajna means "beyond wisdom" and is located between the eyebrows and includes the pituitary gland, eyes, head and lower part of the brain. The Ajna chakra, when open and balanced, helps us to see beyond the material world and into the spirit world and inner world of our intuition. When open, we feel connected to our inner wisdom and sixth sense, and we get regular messages and intuitive hits. When blocked, we may feel confused, discombobulated and searching for answers relentlessly outside of ourselves. To create balance, practice meditation regularly and deep listening to your sixth sense.

Practice the Third Eye chakra mantras here if you'd like, and you're invited to wear or surround yourself with the colors indigo blue and/or violet purple. Sit in meditation more to help yourself turn inward. If there are any questions or situations that you need guidance around, bring those to mind before you meditate, and then pay attention to any visions, thoughts, or ideas that come.

Listen to the music for the Wise Woman, or sit in the silence and just allow it to be a potent space of going within to hear your own inner voice.

Third Eye Chakra Mantras:
I see the unseen.
I am intuitive and wise.
I know what I know.

"All that you are seeking is also seeking you. If you lie still, sit still, it will find you. It has been waiting for you a long time."
~ Clarissa Pinkola Estes

Chapter 9

The Conscious Feminine Leader Archetype: Lead from Love, Inspire a New Way

Crown Chakra

"The world is calling for conscious feminine leadership, where women are leading from balance, strength, and wholeness within themselves. Not motivated by fear and competition, but from a fierce loving desire to create sustainability and collaboration with all life on earth: with men, women, and all our planet's creatures. Now, and for all generations to come."
~ Laura J. Swan

We now move into the energy of service and giving back to the world. When you reclaim your power and come home to yourself as a woman, you may also discover that you feel a calling to help serve and support the world. Perhaps you feel called to help other women find healing as you have, or serve any area of the world that needs your heart. This may very well be a very big reason why you are here on this earth. Connecting to your inner Conscious

Feminine Leader allows you to take all that you have learned and experienced in life and channel it into a calling to serve and help others. This looks differently for all of us, but likely service is something you feel drawn to if you have been called to this pathway. We have moved through some very big and potent energies up to this point that are related to reclaiming parts of ourselves perhaps left behind in the past, and here in the Feminine Leader archetype, we step into how we can take all of who we are and use our lives to serve a higher purpose and greater good.

Who Is She?

The Conscious Feminine Leader (from here on known as the Feminine Leader for simplicity) is a woman who is devoted to using her own life and gifts for the betterment of humanity. Whether it be as a teacher, healer, lightworker, or however her leadership is expressed, she lets her life be an example for others. She is helping to shift the consciousness on this planet through a commitment to shifting her own consciousness. She leads from Love, and not fear, and lets her heart be her guide for all that she takes action on in the world. She is fierce, loving, powerful and resilient. She is willing to be vulnerable and open in her healing process to allow others to be inspired by her journey, rather than feeling she needs to hide her life's struggles or hardships from the world. She embodies her work in the world and walks her talk as best as she can.

She is committed to healing herself, and knows that in doing this, she is helping to heal the world in the most genuine and authentic way. She feels a desire to connect with other leaders and light-workers to collaborate and work together, because she knows that working together is far more powerful than being in competition. She sees a world that works for everyone. She is able to hold this vision in her heart to stay motivated when the mission can seem daunting and overwhelming. She lets Spirit, God, the Goddess, Universal Energy work THROUGH her and AS her. She knows it is not her work alone to help save the world. She allows the Divine to work through her in her leadership, or else she will become burned out by the magnitude of her mission that she feels called to express in this life.

The Shadow Side:

The Feminine Leader can also become so identified with saving the world, or with outer success and approval from others, that she forgets to care for the basic needs of her own life. When out of balance, she puts so much emphasis on her outer leadership that she does not maintain the details of her own life, like close relationships, family and her health. She may get sick, overwhelmed, or be met with a personal crisis that forces her to put life back into a more sustainable balance. Because the Feminine Leader is here to help teach sustainability and balance for the world, if her inner life and personal world is not a reflection of this, it will start to become glaringly apparent and eventually take its toll.

Likely these are the times she must go within and embrace the messiness of her own life and do whatever it takes to come back into balance once again. She is fueled by the love and support in her life and her spiritual connection to a Higher Power or greater calling. If she gets disconnected from this, and identifies too much with her ego or success rather than her deepest calling and mission, her leadership and success will become more and more out of alignment with her heart. She must do what it takes to come back into alignment and find her "north star" once again. In doing so, she will come back to the true calling of why she's here and what she's here to do.

The other shadow side of the feminine leader is losing faith in her ability to bring about a new way. Because she is here to create a new consciousness for the planet, and birthing a new path for humanity, she may feel lost or unsure of how to do this effectively. She may feel alone, overwhelmed or scared that she is not enough She may doubt that she is really cut out for this type of global calling. She may doubt that her feminine qualities of compassion and sensitivity are really her strength because they may feel like a hindrance or too much at times.

Because she is bravely paving a feminine way of being that is a road less traveled, or not yet traveled at all for some in the world, she must always come back to her inner guidance and connection to Spirit so that she knows it is not hers to do alone, but rather her life is being used by Spirit. If she forgets this, she will lose sight of her true power she holds inside. When she takes time to reconnect to this truth, she knows she will never be alone or misguided, or be inadequate or unqualified to do her work in the world. She has everything she needs within her to lead from love and change the world.

Why Reclaim Her?

The Feminine Leader is being called forth on this planet like never before in human history because let's face it... we need her now more than ever. Those of us who feel called to make a difference for humanity are being summoned because our feminine gifts are precious and powerful. They are exactly what the world needs in order to come back into a balance that is sustainable and lasting. Feminine Leaders are strong, yet sensitive ... compassionate, yet fierce. We use our gifts of empathy and love to make a difference rather than our power and force. We have done our own work and experienced our own healing. We can relate to the pain and suffering of the world through our own experience.

We are being asked to fully reclaim the power of our own hearts because our world faces challenges in all areas... from environmental, to social, to economic and more. Feminine Leaders feel the calling to do their part to help uplift the world through sharing our gifts. We need feminine heart-centered wisdom like never before, the type of leadership that cares for all life on this planet and the many generations to come. Our species and this planet are facing irreversible damage if we don't all come together to create a new world that works for everyone. The Feminine Leader feels the call to lead the charge on this transformation for all of humanity.

But we have to embrace our gifts fully, and recognize that we need help in order to carry forth this mission. We can't do it alone. It requires us to fully reclaim our gifts as women and use them for the transformation of the world. We can no longer see our sensitivity, vulnerability or emotionality as a burden, but rather use it as a force for good and healing on the planet. We have to embrace that we all have unique and powerful gifts to share and take a stand collectively that women be treated as equal and powerful forces for good in the world.

When You Are Connected to Your Healthy Inner Feminine Leader:

You feel on fire for your mission and know you are here for a very important cause. You feel the intensity of the world inside you. At times it may move you to tears, anger, or frustration, but ultimately you know that it's because you are so connected to the suffering of the world and you are committed to doing something about it. And this is your superpower. When you embrace your role as a Conscious Feminine Leader, you know that feeling your feelings intensely is a part of the mission. It fuels your ability to be a vulnerable, great leader for others.

You create enough balance in your life to make sure your needs are met and your true self is expressed. From here, you are in a place of congruence and harmony within yourself so that you can best inspire and offer that to others through your work. When you do get out of balance, you know you don't have to hide or make yourself wrong. Your consistent willingness to go within and heal yourself, to make things right in your own life, is actually a demonstration of your leadership and healing of the world as well. You know you don't have to hide your true self or your pain or challenges; these parts of yourself are relatable and powerful for the world to see.

You stand strong and confident in all of who you are. You listen always to the calling and connection in your Soul to Spirit. You stay connected to your sisters, your tribe and other leaders and are uplifted in your work through your willingness to collaborate and connect with like-minded leaders. You are guided every day by your calling and mission. You know you are supported by a superpower team of seen and unseen lightworkers every step of the way. You let Spirit, God, the Goddess move THROUGH you and empower your work in the world every day.

> *"Ours is not the task of fixing the entire world all at once,*
> *but of stretching out to mend the part of the world*
> *that is within our reach."*
> ~ Clarissa Pinkola Estes

Suggested Practices to Cultivate and Connect to Your Inner Feminine Leader:

Find a spiritual practice that allows you to take time away from your active life. This could be any form of meditation that puts you in a place of receptivity and listening. Listen deeply to the stirrings and callings of your Soul. You will receive guidance in these times of quiet stillness about how Spirit wants to move through you and use your life for the Highest Good. Pay attention to your own life's struggles. You will likely find that your unique calling for how you are meant to lead and inspire others will come to you through paying attention to your own life's deepest challenges and struggles. Paying attention to how you have found your way will very much be the key to your greatest gifts and offerings for how you can help others do the same.

Find a cause you believe in, any cause that you feel passionate about, and commit time to creating awareness around this cause. Support furthering this cause in the world with your time and energy. Spend time with other leaders who inspire you and surround yourself with people who you feel aligned with in your visions, missions, and passions. Find your tribe and love them hard. Women leaders need each other very much, because we understand the complexity of this type of multi-passionate and multi-faceted life better than anyone else. We uplift each other to the next level of our gifts naturally just by being in each other's presence.

"In every community, there is work to be done. In every nation, there
are wounds to heal. In every heart, there is the power to do it. "
~ Marianne Williamson

Examples of Archetypes that can fall within the CFL Archetype:
The High Priestess
The Healer
The Entrepreneur
The Mentor/Coach
The Lightworker
The Visionary
The Mystic
The Teacher
The Creatrix
The Sacred Activist
The Leader
*and many more

Historical or Contemporary Examples:

Indira Gandhi: the world's longest-serving female Prime Minister
of India
Lynne Twist: humanitarian, activist, author of Soul of Money and
founder of the Pachamama Alliance
Marianne Williamson: author, activist, spiritual teacher
Jean Shinoda Bolen, MD: psychiatrist, author, teacher of archetypal
psychology
Claire Zammit: expert transformational teacher, leader, mentor and
successful conscious entrepreneur
Vivian Glyck: founder of Just like my Child and the Girl Power
Project

Kathe Schaaf: founder of Gather the Women, author, speaker, psychotherapist

Tanya Lynn: author, founder of Sistership Circle International

"Leaders are called to humility because they know they did not invent their position of power, but are called to employ it for the common good."
~ Matthew Fox

Affirmations to Help Reclaim Your Inner Feminine Leader:
As I heal myself, I help heal the world.
Vulnerability is my superpower.
I follow the calling in my soul to create a better world.
I commit to be of service to humanity at this time.
I am a channel for love and light in this world.
I am guided by a Higher Power and am never alone.
I am surrounded by a circle of lightworkers who empower and uplift my mission.
I have unconditional support, both seen and unseen, to fulfill my mission and calling.

Music to Invoke the Conscious Feminine Leader Archetype:
Panchadasi by Mother Medicine
Everybody Got Their Something by Nikka Costa
I Am Light by India Arie
Love, Serve, and Remember by Kathy Zavada
I Will Be Light by Matisyahu
I Am Woman by Helen Reddy
Crown of Creation by Jonathan Goldman

Storytime ~ How I Reclaimed My Own Inner Conscious Feminine Leader:

At age twenty-five, when I was living in San Diego had been doing my own healing work for a couple of years, I discovered the book Eating in the Light of the Moon. This book was written by the woman I mentioned earlier in Chapter 1 who eventually became a mentor and dear friend to me, Dr. Anita Johnston. After I found her book and read it ALL NIGHT LONG on a full moon lunar eclipse, I felt a calling deep within my soul to host a women's workshop based on the healing I had experienced so far in myself over the previous few years, and on the things I discovered in that book. I had already led women's groups and circles since I was sixteen years old in high school, but after reading this book, I felt a next level of my calling to be a leader and healer emerging. But I was still a little scared to claim it and step into it fully.

Without any expectation that she would actually get back to me, I reached out via email to Anita, a famous author, speaker, psychologist, and world-renowned expert in her field, and told her how much I loved her book. I asked her if she wanted to come lead a workshop with me. To my utter surprise, she wrote me back within five minutes and said "YES! I would love to!" It was absolutely a moment of divine synchronicity and miracles, because she didn't know a thing about me. I had virtually no experience to lead and teach at the level that she was at that time. I felt instantly unworthy and unprepared, and also so excited I nearly peed my pants.

Anita came and we did lead a workshop together. We did it in a women's circle style and format rather than a traditional teaching workshop, as this was what she felt was most effective and powerful for women (and she was right). Leading up to it I had to face many many deep fears and doubts about myself, and whether or not I was ready for that level of leading and facilitating women. I had barely scratched the surface to heal myself! How was I going to help other women?? I got nearly sick thinking of speaking in front of everyone, and felt like a total fraud up there as a "teacher."

But the moment it all changed was when we first opened the workshop. We were standing, twenty to thirty women, in circle. We were doing an opening invocation ritual to set a safe and sacred space for the day, singing a particular chant, *"Love, Serve and Remember"* by John Astin. I looked around the room and felt something so powerful within me, it shook me to the core.

As I looked around I realized that no matter what my history had been, or how many mistakes I had made, or how inexperienced I was, that I had something powerful to share with other women... and we all needed each other to be strong and lead one another urgently. We had all come to "Love, Serve and Remember" and it hit me hard the role I was meant to play in that.

That day I had a chance to speak and share my own vulnerable story. I saw the profound healing effect it had on me and my sisters who were there. I felt the urgent call from the Spirit of life itself, from God, to get over my fears, to be raw and vulnerable with women and meet them on the same level, and step into serving and leading them NOW – not in ten or twenty years when I felt I was healed and educated and more experienced. I felt that I would be guided and supported by this Divine Force in all I did, and that it would never be my work alone.

I looked around at the women there in circle with me, so many of them with the same stories and heartaches I had been through, so many who had suffered and survived many hardships… and none of us were any better than the others. We were sisters. We were leaders. We were healers. All of us. And the more we have looked within the darkness of our own Soul, the more we are able to relate to and help others, too. I felt the deepest core calling I had ever felt that I was meant to lead and inspire other women to come home to the truth of who they are, and lead their lives from love and wholeness, because that was what I was committed to doing myself. And we were all in it together.

I felt the profound effect that being in circle with other women in this way had on me and on all those who were there. I knew I was meant to speak, write and lead women's circles and workshops from that point on for the rest of my life (even though it scared me to death). I felt that day the anchoring of my inner Conscious Feminine Leader and chose to allow my pain and past and fears and doubts to actually be a catalyst for changing the future of our planet for many generations to come. I knew I could no longer afford to use my fear or self-doubt as an excuse that I wasn't ready, or not good enough. I was needed, we all were. I knew I had to get myself out of the way to just show up and follow the calling from God in my heart once and for all.

Of course in the many years since then, I have wavered in my confidence and trust in myself. Each new level I have had to rise to in my leadership, business, and life provides new levels of fear and self-doubt to face. But I always go back to that moment in time... when I had that moment of knowing within myself of my purpose and my calling... and I allow it to inspire me to get myself out of the way so I can LEAD from LOVE and trust, rather than from fear and doubt.

Questions for Reflection:

What feelings or emotions get activated inside you through exploring this archetype? How have you felt called to lead and share your gifts? Where have you held yourself back out of fear of not being ready or experienced enough? What's one way you feel called to step into your leadership right now? How can you take action on that calling this week?

The 7th Chakra: Sahasrara or Crown
Colors: Pink, White
Element: Consciousness
Seed Sound: AUM or Silence
Stones to Help Balance: Selenite, Clear Quartz,
Diamond, Rose Quartz

The physical location of the crown chakra is on the crown of the head, and the organs associated are the pineal gland, nervous system, and the pituitary gland. The Crown Chakra represents our connection to the Divine and is our portal to our highest consciousness. It is our connection to our calling to be of service to the world. It is where we source a more conscious way of thinking, and draw upon wisdom from a Higher Power greater than our minds or ego alone. When open and balanced, you feel guided by Spirit, connected to your purpose, and aligned with God's will in your life. When imbalanced or closed, you may feel alone and inadequate to fulfill your mission. You may feel like you are "doing it all alone" and exhausted and depleted because of this.

Practice the mantras provided here, and let it be a sacred time to connect to your mission and the calling you feel in this life. If you are still discovering it, open to the possibility of this being a meditation to help you discover it more fully. Imagine your Crown Chakra being filled with light from ray above you, like a light pink or golden shower, and allow it to move through you throughout your entire body. Let yourself create from this place as you take action throughout your day, as if you are being moved by something greater than yourself. You are invited to wear or surround yourself with pink, whites, or gold, and listen to the music provided in this section if you want to get inspired for your Divine Feminine Mission in this life.

Crown Chakra Mantras:

I surrender my will for Thy will.
I open to Divine Guidance to share my gifts.
I am a channel for Love…use me.

"…In my uttermost bones I know something, as do you. It is that there can be no despair when you remember why you came to Earth, who you serve, and who sent you here.

The good words we say and the good deeds we do are not ours. They are the words and deeds of the One who brought us here. In that spirit, I hope you will write this on your wall: When a great ship is in harbor and moored, it is safe, there can be no doubt. But that is not what great ships are built for."

~ Excerpt from *You Were Made for These Times*
By Clarissa Pinkola Estes

Chapter 10

The Creatrix Archetype: Unleash Your Feminine Power

All Chakras

"Tell me ... what is it you plan to do with your one wild and precious life?"
~ Mary Oliver

At last we have arrived at the Creatrix archetype. The Creatrix within us is a connection to our full creative potential. When we reclaim our power and honor all of who we are – honoring each part of ourselves that longs to be expressed – she naturally comes forth. When we embrace our Creatrix, we are stepping into our full feminine power from our wholeness, with no part of ourselves left behind. The Creatrix invites us to accept all of who we are, and uses both the darkness and the light we have experienced in life to birth our beauty and magic. She allows us to create our vision for the world because she has access to incredible resources within and all around us. She represents us as women being lit up, activated, and connected to our full potential. We are creating from a place of authentic power – which as women, is deeply rooted in our Love and wisdom.

Who Is She?

The Creatrix Archetype is the representation of our full creative and life force potential as women. She is often personified as fertility deities or goddesses, or goddesses of the harvest or earth. Her essence is felt in the Great Mother goddesses, the Earth goddesses, as well as the Artistic/Creative goddesses, and represents our magnificent, magical ability to create and birth new life in this world... from children, to projects, to art, to music, to love. She is the fertile creative, life-giving power within all beings, and fuels the birth and growth of all things. She holds the power to create anything she desires, and knows her full magic and abilities to do this. She is tapped into an infinite well of resources. Her power comes from the infinite source of ALL life and Creation. She is represented in this pathway and journey by the symbol of the spiral, as the spiral represents the cycles of constant evolution, death and rebirth, and infinite feminine creative energy.

Another side of the Creatrix, perhaps a misunderstood and challenging side for some, is her power to destroy life and to clear away what is not serving in order for new life to be made possible. She knows what must die in order for life to thrive. She is able to sacrifice the old to make way for the new. This is the part of the Creatrix that is equally as powerful as birthing new life, but difficult to embrace because of our own judgments and challenges around letting go of what is no longer meant to be.

She is intimately connected to the cycles of nature, and the death and rebirth cycle that is persistent and prevalent in all of nature (and all of life!). There is a time to be alive and create (spring, summer) and a time to let die and go within (fall, winter). This is why the Creatrix is intimately connected to the Moon and the Moon's mystery and magic. The Moon's twenty-eight-day cycle is often connected to and compared to women's menstrual cycles. Our menstrual cycle is representative of, and necessary for, our womb to conceive and birth life in the world. The very cycle in our bodies that creates life in the world requires a bleeding and shedding of our womb each month to make way for the new possibility of an egg to be fertilized and implanted. This could not happen if we didn't bleed and release the old. Similarly, the Moon goes into total darkness and quiet each month with the New Moon, and then emerges again in her fullness and light each month without fail as the Full Moon. So, does the Creatrix, allowing times of darkness, death, and stillness so that the fullness of light and life can emerge.

The Shadow Side:

One shadow side of the Creatrix (if we are not connected to her power) is that we feel disconnected from our creative magic and from our ability to have influence in the direction of our own destiny. We may think we have no power in creating our own happiness and feel that life is completely out of our control. We may have challenges in our fertility and reproductive systems and feel this is a sign that we are not fertile creatures (which could not be further from the truth). We may feel like we are not a "real woman" if we have not yet been able to, or have not chosen to, conceive or birth children, and therefore we disconnect from this archetype altogether. We may think that we have to be mothers in order to be fertile and nurturing new life.

The other shadow side, if we are not able to embrace the destroyer aspect of the Creatrix, is that we feel guilt and shame around letting things die or transmute to a new form. Or we may feel complete resistance to change and allowing the Creatrix to clear the path for what is wanting to birth. We may feel resistant to ending a relationship, or leaving a job, or letting go of old addictions or patterns. We do not let the Creatrix come in and offer her gifts to destroy what is no longer serving us. We may judge ourselves or curse God, and feel like life is against us. If we go through a crisis or breakup or loss that levels us, rather than seeing it as the Creatrix at work in her magic, we may see it as a sign that God has abandoned us, or that we are doing something "wrong" and are being punished. This also could not be further from the truth. The power of the Creatrix lies also in her ability to rip away what we are not willing to remove ourselves, and often this can bring us to our knees.

"And the day came when the risk to remain tight in a bud was more painful than the risk it took to blossom."
~ Anais Nin

Why Reclaim Her?

Reclaiming the Creatrix means reclaiming the full power of your feminine creative potential... and this is no small thing. It means owning that you have the power within your body, mind, heart to create a life that is aligned with your Soul, and a world around us that is aligned with your Truth. Sometimes this is too much responsibility to take on. For many of us as women, we are stuck in a belief system that puts the power of our destiny out onto someone else in the world. We don't realize how powerful and magnificent we truly are. This holds us back from using our creative potential to create the life of our dreams.

Collectively and individually, women are rising into a more fully expressed version of ourselves and realizing our power. We are letting the old paradigm of the disempowerment of women die, because it is no longer serving us or the world (and let's be real, it never was). Embracing our Creatrix inside means rising to the fullest potential of what you can create in this life. It is an invitation to own ALL of you... to let ALL of your energies and archetypes be expressed, so that you are working with a full capacity and operating from your wholeness.

You can be a mother, healer, leader, CEO, artist, wise woman, or any combination of these expressions... and be in your full creative potential and power. You don't have to choose just one, or limit your life to any particular role. Again, reclaiming your Creatrix means reclaiming ALL of you, and likely you are a multi-passionate and complex woman with many parts of herself longing to be expressed. When you reclaim and empower yourself as the Creatrix, you are reclaiming your fertility on all levels. If you are trying to conceive or create a baby, the place to start is proclaiming that you are a fertile woman in more ways than one. You are fertile in a million ways. This realization will inevitably support the act of creation in all areas of your body, mind and heart.

Reclaiming the Creatrix also means reclaiming and embracing both the darkness and the light within you, with no parts left behind. The parts of you that have had to die so the new could come forth, the parts of you that made mistakes so you could grow and learn, the parts of you that tried to create something new and miserably failed, the parts of you that have been hurt or abused... all of this is embraced within the Creatrix cycle of death and rebirth. No part of you is outside the realm of your beauty and perfection. This is again represented in the spiral and our shape of emergence that symbolizes constant evolution. As the Creatrix, you are leaning into the darkness, then back into the light. Each cycle you become more deeply connected to your authentic truth.

"When I understood and accepted my own darkness,
I was consumed by my own light."
~ Unknown

When You Are Connected to Your Healthy Inner Creatrix:

You are powerful, alive, activated, and centered. You know you have the power to create your life. You know you must surrender to a Higher Power that is greater than you and a great mystery that sometimes you may not understand (but you trust it). You move through creative cycles of death and rebirth, and you are able to let life move through you like the powerful spiral symbol of creative life force energy. You ride the spiral of life around the bends and curves, up and down, into the darkness and back into the light, knowing that you will always emerge more powerful and alive than the last cycle. You trust in this cycle of death and rebirth in your own life.

You are able to dance between your different roles and responsibilities without feeling like you have multi-personality disorder. You see your multi-passionate life as a gift that feeds your soul. You embrace your complexity and do your best to create balance between all your passions so that you can show up fully in each area of your life. You embrace the range of your experiences and embrace them all as a part of being alive, a part of being human, and a part of being fully willing to let life in rather than shut it down. You surrender and let die what is no longer meant to be, and you ride the waves of grief, sadness and anger as a part of this loss. But you also do so knowing what is emerging underneath the surface. You live your life from trust in all of Creation and in the Divine's plan for your life. You Create from a place of knowing who you are and what you are capable of in this life. You are the CREATRIX.

Suggested Practices to Cultivate and Connect to Your Inner Creatrix:

Get connected to your body through movement and dance that lights you up. Move regularly, and allow music to be a part of your physical activity. Track your fertility cycles (if you are having them, or if you are wanting to become more fertile to conceive a baby) and pay attention to when you are ovulating. Women sometimes experience their cycles of creativity and energy are very much affected by their fertility cycle; getting more connected to yours can enhance your creative energy overall.

Pay attention to the moon cycles, and watch how your cycles are connected to them by journaling each month on the New Moon and Full Moon. During each New Moon, plant seeds of intentions and share your desires and wishes for what you want to create. Take stock of what perhaps may need to be cleared away so that the new seeds can be planted. Be willing to make changes if necessary.

During each Full Moon, celebrate and give thanks for your manifestations each month. Honor what you have created in your life thus far. Pay attention to what is "illuminated" during the time of the Full Moon as you look at what you are creating, and make adjustments as necessary to keep yourself on track for your desires, goals, and manifestations.

Trust your DESIRE and trust what you are longing for is longing for you too. Know that all of creation begins with the power of this desire within you, and you are not wrong to want what you want in this life. Trust in your creative power to bring it forth through integrating all of your capacities, energy centers, and archetypes that we have cultivated thus far. Embrace your WHOLENESS.

> *"You are the Universe*
> *And there ain't nothin' you can't do*
> *If you conceive it, you can achieve it*
> *That's why, I believe in you, yes I do."*
> ~ From the song *"You are the Universe"*
> by The Brand New Heavies

Examples of the Creatrix Archetype:

In Mythology and Stories:

Yemaja: from African origins, the Mother Goddess of the ocean, fertility, and the source of the sun and moon (and much more).

Ixchel: in Mayan mythology, the goddess of fertility and creativity, the protector of women and childbirth, goddess who gave birth to all the world

Freya: in Norse mythology, the goddess of fertility, magic, and creativity.

Pele: the goddess of fire, death and rebirth, lightning, and volcanoes in Hawaiian mythology.

Kali: goddess of endings and beginnings, and Mother of the Universe in Hindu mythology

Historical or Contemporary Examples:

Clarissa Pinkola Estés: American poet, Jungian psychoanalyst, post-trauma recovery specialist, author and spoken word artist

Marion Woodman, PhD: Canadian mythopoetic author, women's movement figure, and Jungian analyst

Laura Hollick: Soul Art Shaman, creative spiritual entrepreneur, lover of the Earth

Sara Avant Stover: author, speaker, feminine empowerment leader

Isabella Konold: muse of the agony and ecstasy of life, speaker, performance artist

"There is a vitality, a life-force, an energy, a quickening that is translated through you into action, and because there is only one of you in all of time this expression is unique. And if you block it, it will never exist through any other medium and be lost. The world will not have it! It is not your business to determine how good it is nor how it compares with other expressions. It is your business to keep it yours clearly and directly, to keep the channel open."
~ Martha Graham

Affirmations to Help Reclaim Your Inner Creatrix:
I hold the source of all life within me.
I am unlimited creative potential.
I have the power to create the life of my dreams every day.
My body is a vessel to birth new life in all ways.
My feminine power fully alive and activated.
I embrace the darkness as potent and powerful for my growth.
I create beauty, magic, and love in this world.
I surrender what needs to die so that the new can come forth.
I give birth to all of myself.
I embrace my wholeness and all parts of myself.
I am the CREATRIX.

Music to Invoke the Creatrix Archetype:
Existence by Shylah Ray Sunshine (Featuring Mother Medicine)
I'm Every Woman by Chaka Khan
You Are the Universe by The Brand New Heavies
I've Got the Power by Snap
The Gifts of the Goddess by Karen Drucker
Devi Prayer by Craig Pruess & Ananda
Gayatri Mantra by Deva Premal

"Without darkness, nothing comes to birth.
As without light, nothing flowers."
~ May Sarton

Storytime ~ How I Reclaimed My Own Inner Creatrix:

I have come to know the power of the Creatrix within me through experiencing each and every archetype we have explored here. To me, she is the expression of full feminine power and creative energy, and a power that emerges from embracing all parts of ourselves, both the darkness and the light, and utilizing all the internal resources at our disposal. I've discovered a different aspect of her throughout many different experiences in life.

With each death and loss, I felt a new aspect of my powerful Creatrix rise from the ashes... as well as with each birth and new life I have brought forth.

In my time living in Hawaii, I learned about a very powerful goddess named Pele. Pele is the volcano goddess of death, destruction, and fire... but also the goddess of all creation and rebirth. According to Hawaiian mythology, her violent volcanic eruptions that rose up from the seabed floor gave birth to the mountains that became the pristine Hawaiian Islands. And this is literally true in the sense that the soil that is created from the lava of volcanic eruptions is the most fertile, nutrient dense soil on earth. It is fertile grounds for luscious plants and rainforests to grow abundantly. And this is why Hawaii is so ridiculously beautiful and special... it literally was birthed from volcanoes erupting up from the sea floor.

I learned that Pele has the power to both destroy with her fire, as well as give birth to endlessly beautiful islands. And she most certainly does both. Hawaiian mythology also says that Pele lives in the Halemaumau Crater at the summit of Kilauea Volcano on the Big Island, also known as the Navel of the World where the gods began creation. She is said to be very happy there, but Hawaiians also warn of the importance of having great respect for her power. She is generous and kind and beautiful, but she is also fierce and not afraid to let die what needs to die. You definitely don't want to piss off Madame Pele and be under her wrath, say the Hawaiians.

While living on the Big Island, as I have shared already, I had many powerful healing experiences. When I first arrived there, I had a lot of shadows and darkness to look at within myself. I had been running, literally, every day in Boston to try to avoid feeling anything intensely. When I got to the Islands, I was literally and metaphorically stuck on an island with nowhere to run. I couldn't avoid parts of myself that I was able to distract from in a busy, bustling city. I could either get out of there fast to avoid what was coming up, or I could go within myself and do the work. And so... I stayed.

When I learned about Pele, her symbolism struck me. I had been so afraid to look at the mistakes I thought I had made, or the darkness and depression I had inside, and I could not see a blessing in any of the hardships I had endured. I had taken it all out on myself, and I thought I was screwed and flawed for life. But when I came to understand the mythology of Pele and what she represented inside of me, the beauty that could be birthed from such destruction, I came to believe in a new possibility of rebirth within myself.

I became clear that I wanted to transform the relationship with my darkness, and decided to create a ritual for embracing my own shadows that I then enacted many times while living there. I was not far from Volcanoes National Park, where the famous smoldering active Halemaumau volcano crater lies and Madame Pele is said to reside. I decided I would write out each week all the things I wanted to embrace and forgive within myself, all the shadows that were emerging while I was there that I wanted to transmute into healing opportunities. I wrote on a piece of recycled paper in my journal, and let it fill with words and memories each week.

I then periodically would go alone on an epic hike through old lava fields and rainforests in Volcanoes National Park right up to the Halemaumau Crater. At that time, we were allowed to hike right up to the smoking volcano crater's edge (you can't get that close any longer because there is active lava spewing up now) and I would release my piece of paper into the smoking hole where I imagined it was being transmuted into lava. I imagined this lava becoming new land one day and fertile soil for new life to emerge. I didn't have to know how that was going to actually look in my own life, I just had to believe that it was possible. And in time, after repeating this ritual over and over, and in combination with all the other healing elements of this island I experienced, I started to feel a profound shift inside of me.

While in Hawaii, I can say I truly activated the power of the Creatrix within me and connected to her power. It has taken me many years to embody and express her more fully, and I still work on this every day... but on those islands is where my journey began. I started to connect deeply to the moon and the moon's cycles from complete darkness to its full expression. I felt the power of the Creatrix to both take life away, and to birth new life in this world. I came to believe that I too would be able to birth the beauty I desired in the world once again. I began to have a love and compassion for myself that had been missing for many years, and I looked at my past in a new light.

I had not had a menstrual cycle in many years, and was not sure if I would be able to have children. I had been told by two doctors already that likely I would not. While there in Hawaii, I connected to my fertility, my body, and my feminine creative power that was independent of my ability to have children. I knew, even if I never gave birth to physical children through my own womb, I would become a mother in many, many ways, and birth all types of beauty in the world... babies, visions, projects, relationships, and more. I certainly didn't know how all of this was going to happen way back then, but I felt it with all my heart.

As I write this final chapter, I am now eight months pregnant with my second child, a little boy named Maui. I am already the mother of a beautiful little girl named Luna, and I have a husband I adore, and a business empowering women worldwide that is authentic to my heart and Soul. My children's names are a tribute to some of the most healing experiences of my life that have helped to bring them to me... Luna: my connection to the moon and to healing and empowering the feminine energy within myself and this world, and Maui: the name of a Polynesian Sun warrior, a symbol of healing the masculine energy and bringing it into balance within myself and this world, and a reflection of my (and my husband's) love for the Hawaiian Islands that brought me back to life.

I have also had three abortions and two miscarriages, and made many mistakes in life I was not sure I could forgive myself for. I lived with painful, debilitating menstrual periods for most of my life and struggled with countless fertility challenges. I did not know if I would ever be where I am now. But I'm certain I had to believe that I deserved to have the life of my dreams for it all to evolve in time.

Giving birth naturally in my home to my daughter Luna was one of the most empowering experiences of my life. It tapped me into whole new level of strength that I have as a woman to be a bringer of life. I am deeply grateful for the healing process that brought me right up to that day, and that I trusted my inner Wise Woman to guide me every step of the way (even when it was scary). Here, as I sit pregnant with my second child, I am birthing this book (a long-time dream) and a new level of my creative gifts in the world. I am running a successful business empowering women worldwide. I feel my Creatrix fully activated and ignited. But the gifts that I am experiencing now, and the teachings I can now share with other women, are a result of embracing and trusting all that has transpired in my life.

These gifts today are rooted deeply in the fertile soil of my own lava fields of past pain and destruction. Had I not chosen to embrace both the darkness and the light, I would never have been able to create the blessings that I have now, nor would I be able to help others do the same in quite the same way. I had to learn to trust it all, not just the pretty parts. And I had to learn to trust God, to trust myself, and ultimately... to trust every decision I have ever made as being the right one for me at that time.

I believe we ALL have the power to create new life and to rise from the ashes, no matter our age, race, background or our reproductive health status. I have traveled to the jungles of Ecuador, to the deserts of the Middle East, to the villages of Africa... and I have seen this feminine spirit and resilience rising in all women worldwide. It is independent of the choices we have made or the pain of our past. We can allow all of our life to be fertile soil for the creations we desire to birth in the world if we choose. Every single woman is a Creatrix, and we all hold an incredible force of creation within us that is tapped into a wealth of resources. We can draw upon the strength of all the archetypes inside us, and call upon each one as we need to in order to help facilitate the life we want to create. This is the power of the Creatrix I have discovered, and that I continue to cultivate in my life every day. I hope she has been activated within you, too.

Questions for Reflection:

What feelings or emotions are activated through exploring this archetype? Where have you felt the destructive power of this archetype in your life? Where have you experienced her rebirthing energy and resurrection power? What does your inner Creatrix want to create right now in your life? What practices can you commit to in order to call her forth in her full power right now?

ALL CHAKRAS
Color: White, and she has access to the full spectrum
of the rainbow and all colors depending on what
she is creating or birthing
Element: ALL
Seed Sound: ALL
Stones to Help Balance: Combination of all that have
been shared so far

The Creatrix Archetype embodies all the chakras and archetypes fully activated and lit up. She has access to all of her energy centers so she is able to create from a full capacity.

Chakra Mantras for the Creatrix:
I am activated, energized, and open.
I create from my wholeness.
I AM all that I AM.

"As the Great Creatrix, the feminine is no vessel and passage for an alien, masculine Other that condescends towards her, enters into her, and favors her with the seed of living. Life originates in her and issues from her, and the light that appears projected on the night sky, which she is herself, is rooted in her depths. For she is not only the protomantis, the first and great Prophetess, but also she who gives birth to the Spirit-Light, which, like consciousness and the illumination that arises in transformation, is rooted in her creative efficacy. She is the creative Earth, which not only brings forth and swallows life, but as that which transforms also lets the dead thing be resurrected and leads the lower to the higher. All developments and transformations that lead from the simple and insignificant through all gradations of life to the complicated and intricately differentiated fall under her sovereignty. This matriarchal world is geocentric; the stars and signs of the zodiac are the heavenly girdle of the Earth Goddess and are arranged around her as the true center around which everything revolves."

~ Eric Neumann

Chapter 11

Integration and Celebration: Where Do We Go from Here?

"We shall not cease from exploration, and the end of all our exploring will be to arrive where we started and know the place for the first time."
~ T. S. Eliot

Well my sister…you made it!

Congratulations for coming to the end of our creative exploration together, and welcome to the beginning of the next phase of your life.

I hope you have received value from the journaling, suggested practices, and exercises here, and that you are a more whole and empowered woman because of them. I trust that in sharing my own personal journey with you that it has invited an inquiry into your life and made this work very real. I hope together that all of this has been supportive of helping you connect to your highest calling, and to your greatest gifts and power coming forth.

My intention in this journey was to allow you to explore different realms of feminine energies and expressions, and allow you to activate and awaken them within yourself for your own personal power. In doing this, you have access to different parts of yourself as you need them in life. There are moments when you need to call forth your Warrioress to get things done or get through a challenging time that requires you to be at your fullest (on no sleep). Or you need to activate the Mother energy inside you to nurture yourself with love, compassion, and hot tea after a breakup or let down. Or it's time to call forth your Queen and confidence when you need to have a hard conversation and speak your truth. We have all these qualities and energies within us that we can utilize at any time, and the archetypes help give us a face and a name to relate to as we do.

This is not for you to think of yourself as fragmented parts or split personalities, but rather to see that you hold an internal wealth of resources, a team of cohesive parts, that are available at your disposal to help you create the best life imaginable. We all need different strengths, different characteristics, different energies at any given time. And most of us long for expression in more than one area of our lives. Exploring the archetypes in the way we just did will allow you access to MORE of yourself, so you can draw upon who and what you need on any given day or moment and utilize your powerful feminine energy inside you to the fullest.

This pathway of discovering and embracing all parts of yourself is one that has no beginning and no end, but like the spiral, moves through phases and evolutions throughout our whole lives. The archetypes that we explored here are but a few of the range of the energies out there, so I encourage you to keep exploring and keep discovering more about yourself and who you are inside in whatever way you feel called. Celebrate the wonderful work you have done on yourself so far, even if it has brought up difficult questions or had you look at uncomfortable places. This is an inevitable part of growth and change, and your courage to do the work will take you to incredible places, and you will inspire others to do the same.

Because as I have shared, I believe we are at a critical time in human history, and women are a powerful part of shifting our world to a better place. You are a part of this, and we all are a part of this. I know this is not easy, and takes so much strength and courage. And that's also why we need each other as women to remember the truth of who we are... we can't do this alone. We can no longer afford to be in competition or against each other as women. And I believe the more YOU step into your power, the more ALL women will. Together we all can share our gifts with the world, there is no scarcity for any of us. There are like-minded sisters all over the world who will walk side by side with you on this journey, this I know for sure. You just have to set your intention to find them, and you will discover a support system that is far, deep and wide on this planet.

So please also know that we dove into some potent questions and concepts, and these can take time to become integrated into our lives and our way of being every day. So, don't feel like you had to "get it" all here at once! Be gentle with yourself and have patience with your process. Reclaiming our power, and embracing our full creative potential, is a lifelong journey, and we come to new levels of understanding ourselves every day. What matters is that you stay true to yourself and listen to the calling of your heart. You will always be guided to the next right step for you in your path of healing and transformation, whatever that may be.

> *"This above all: to thine own self be true."*
> ~ William Shakespeare

Storytime ~ La Loba Revisited - Singing over the Bones

Our first story of this journey I shared was La Loba, or Wolf Woman. La Loba wandered the deserts looking for the lost and forgotten bones of animals so that she could piece them back toge ther again and make them whole. She left no bone behind, and every part of the animal was sacred in order to reclaim the whole creature. If you recall, after she had gathered all the bones, she then would wait for the perfect song to sing over the fully intact skeleton, and then sing for as long as it took to bring new flesh, new life, and revitalized spirit to the body of what once left behind.

So goes this journey of reclaiming our power as women. We may have to go back and remember the bones from the past, many of which we would rather forget. We may have to reclaim the parts of ourselves that have been left behind, parts that we thought were unworthy of love or respect. We may have to reclaim some of our buried dreams deep inside, some of our creative desires or passionate impulses, that were perhaps at risk of being long forgotten. And it may take wandering the deserts of our internal world for a while, spiraling into the center of being, and then out once again. And it may take courage and conviction to gather each bone, each and every time.

But when we do this, and we take the time to honor each and every part of what has made us who we are, we are reclaiming all of ourselves, and trusting that no mistake or choice or experience has the ability to take away our power, or take away from the truth of who we really are inside. And that is where our true power lies. Then our wild, creative, powerful and passionate spirit can be made whole and truly reborn once again. And when we set her free, she will run laughing into the sunset, full of life, full of joy, full of real and raw experiences that made her who she is. She will embody her wholeness, with no parts left behind.

Thank you for collecting the bones with me. I did so right along with you in sharing my stories and honoring my past in this book. I continue to reclaim myself, bone by bone, as we likely all will forever. And together we will run off into the sunset... laughing, crying, rejoicing... And embracing our true freedom and power as women at last.

The Guest House
This being human is a guest house.
Every morning a new arrival.
A joy, a depression, a meanness,
some momentary awareness comes
as an unexpected visitor.
Welcome and entertain them all!
Even if they are a crowd of sorrows,
who violently sweep your house
empty of its furniture,
still, treat each guest honorably.
He may be clearing you out
for some new delight.
The dark thought, the shame, the malice.
meet them at the door laughing and invite them in.
Be grateful for whatever comes.
because each has been sent
as a guide from beyond.
~ Jellaludin Rumi

Where Do We Go from Here?

I want you to know as we come to the end that I'm here to support you in your continued healing and evolution as a woman. As a women's life and leadership coach, I offer many different ways to empower your wholeness and greatness. As I have shared before, this book is the companion to a full **Reclaim Your Power** women's transformational program online. If you have enjoyed the journey we did here, and want to expand on it more and cultivate yourself in each of the archetypes even more so... I invite you to join this program anytime.

There are options to study it at your own pace in a very simple to use virtual platform, or to join the next live version of the program online and circle with women from all over the world. If this work has touched you or intrigued you, please join us. The **Reclaim Your Power** online program expands upon all that we have done here, and guides you through experiential exercises to help you more fully embody each archetype and concept. This work has empowered women all over the world to find their voice, awaken to their gifts, and step into their leadership and full potential. I trust if you feel drawn to it, it will support you, too.

"Seek more opportunities to put more Love in the world."
~ Marianne Williamson

If you are feeling called to lead and inspire others, and are ready to get started NOW, I have a program called Lead from Love: A course in Conscious Feminine Leadership for Today's Visionary Women. If you feel called to step into your role as a leader, healer, coach, speaker, and/or teacher, or you want to start facilitating women's programs and circles yourself, I invite you to explore this program. We move through the archetypes of Conscious Feminine Leadership, many of which we touched on here in this book within that chapter, and allow you to find your own authentic form of YOUR feminine leadership at this time. You will emerge more confident and on fire for your mission than ever before, and have a tribe of like-minded women around you to empower your vision to the fullest.

I also have in depth personal coaching programs, as well as a Creatrix Mastermind women's group that is offered once a year to empower your creative dreams with a tribe of like-minded sisters by yours side.

If you enjoyed reading about my stories in Hawaii, and would like to have a mind-blowing experience there of your own, then join us for the next Creatrix Activation retreat. I take women out to Hawaii on a guided journey of healing, empowerment, and creative activation that is inspired by my own healing experiences out there and my connection to the islands. The retreats are out of this world magical, and we would love to have you join us for the next one.

You can find out about all that I offer at my website: *LaurajSwan.com*, and you'll find many free goodies and gifts for you there as well. I am honored to have been your guide on this journey, and to share my story with you as you explore your own. I hope I can play a role in supporting you more in the future.

With all my love,
Laura J. Swan
Xo

As we come to the end of our journey, I will leave you with a few questions to help you integrate all that we covered, and ground into this new way of being that you have invited through this exploration:

Integration and Celebration - Questions for Reflection:

1. What were some of the most impactful realizations I have had from my Reclaim Your Power journey? What has stood out as a big "ah-ha" or shift in my perspective?

2. What archetypes were the most empowering for me? And which were the most triggering or challenging? Why?

3. Based on what I have discovered, what do I most want to transform and change in my life? What am I ready to let go of? What needs to "die" so that my newly reclaimed, true self can step forth?

4. What do I want to create with my life from here on? What am I truly ready to embrace about myself and my power that I had not been ready to before? What do I truly DESIRE to birth with this one wild and precious life I have been given?

Mantras for Integration and Celebration:
I Remember who I am, and how I have come to be here.
I Reclaim my feminine wisdom and allow it to lead my life.
I Rebirth my life from my true feminine power
and wholeness today.

What Is Success?

To laugh often and much;
To win the respect of intelligent people
and the affection of children;
To earn the appreciation of honest critics
and endure the betrayal of false friends;
To appreciate beauty;
To find the best in others;
To leave the world a bit better, whether by
a healthy child, a garden patch
or a redeemed social condition;
To know even one life has breathed
easier because you have lived;

This is to have succeeded.

~ Ralph Waldo Emerson

Epilogue

In the course of writing this book, I went through a remarkable transformation. Not just emotionally and spiritually, but literally and physically as well. The book that you have read up to this point was to be written, published and released in an online book launch by September 6, 2017. As you read in the Creatrix Chapter, I was eight to nine months pregnant as I finished this book. I was fully connected to the Creatrix Archetype within me, birthing many creations all at once. And I had the perfect plan for how I was going to release them BEFORE my baby came.

My son, Maui Jonathan Budd, was due on September 30th, 2017, so September 6 felt like a wonderful "birthday" for my book to come out before my real baby was born. Well... as John Lennon said, "Life is what happens to you while you're busy making other plans," and that was most certainly true in my case.

On the eve of the original launch date for the book you're holding now, my son Maui was born, and I had an incredibly empowering homebirth just like I had with my daughter Luna. He was three weeks early, and was most definitely a big surprise showing up long before his due date. My first reaction to seeing my water break at 4:00 am that morning was panic and confusion. Could this really be happening? Is he healthy and OK coming so early? How would this affect my carefully laid out plans? How would this affect my book launch? How am I going to reschedule everything that I had committed to this week???

But then suddenly my contractions started and it became clear what was happening, I stopped and prayed. My husband and I connected and shared our fears. I was being thrust into the Mother Archetype much more intensely and quickly than I thought, birthing another baby and going into the newborn phase on a timeline I had not planned. And yet it was happening, so I realized I had a choice. Do I constrict and go into fear? Or do I trust and allow it to be as it is, trusting in life and trusting in my body's wisdom right now?

So, I chose trust. I chose to believe that my body was incredibly wise and knew exactly what she was doing, as did my son. And this allowed me to go into my twelve-hour homebirth experience with total peace, calm, and trust. It turned out to be the most empowering experience of my life, and I felt myself connected to a long lineage of mamas giving birth for eons in this way. If I had been in fear and anxiety about my plans not going as I hoped, I would certainly never have been able to receive the fullness of the experience as I did.

I did have to cancel my original book launch, and many other things. But birthing him right when I did has also birthed a whole new part of myself that is priceless beyond words. His arrival has brought forth another level of Love, and of my own feminine power and strength, that I could only have realized through birthing and loving him. And it has all worked out as it should.

I chose to trust life, and to trust what archetype was called forth in the timing that it was for me. I write this now as my son is two and a half weeks old, and I have to say he came in absolute perfect timing. I have been in full on new mama mode, and that has taken all of me to care for him. I can't believe I found the time to write this Epilogue!! I am not in book launch mode at all, and yet I'm trusting in the perfection of his arrival with all my heart as I share this book with the world, too. He will now likely be present in my arms at my online book launch, as he should be. After all… he did co-author this book with me for months, and he deserves to celebrate its release as much as I do.

I share this final story with you as an example that we as women can be true to ourselves in our careers and offerings for the world as well as be devoted mothers. I believe we can have it all, maybe not all at the same moment, and maybe it will be messy and unpredictable, but we can create a life that allows us as women to be mothers AND devoted to our careers and passions. Because the world needs all of this from us… our gifts to serve our purpose, as well as our loving, mothering qualities to raise beautiful children. We just have to be willing to value all of our offerings and all of ourselves fully, and not think that we are unworthy of sharing any part of our gifts. We also have to be OK with imperfection as we do it, and not let that hold us back.

My career is taking a back seat right at this very moment in time because I'm nursing a baby every two hours around the clock and sleeping very little. My hormones are adjusting and fluctuating every day, and I'm responsible for caring for a very active three-year-old toddler and being a good mommy to her as well. It is not easy at all right now… sometimes I think I'm going to lose it! AND… I'm totally embracing and enjoying this time here and now because it will never come again. I'm being gentle with myself, and giving myself permission to feel it all. The struggle and the love. The challenge and the joy. Life will come back into more balance in due time, and in the meantime, I'm fully embracing the archetype that is being called forth in me while trusting the others will have their time to shine again soon.

So, I have found a few minutes as my baby sleeps here next to me and my daughter is running in circles in the back yard to share this message with you. I want to give you hope and inspiration that if you have a gift to give and a message to share with the world... don't let anything hold you back. It may take longer and be a hell of a lot more difficult if you are a full-time mom, or working for Corporate America, or a full-time student, but don't let anyone or anything take away your dream, or hold you back from what you know you're here to do. Trust yourself, trust your gifts, and trust the Divine timing of life. You are here for great things, sister. You are a powerful Creatrix. Anything you dream of in your heart is possible. I believe in you, and I know sometimes it's hard. But we are all meant to experience our wholeness and power, and though this looks different for everyone, it is possible for all of us.

Xo
With all my love,
Laura

About the Author
Laura J. Swan, M.A., E-RYT, CHLC

Laura is a devoted wife and mother, a women's life and leadership coach, an intuitive healer, and a passionate advocate of women's healing, leadership, and empowerment on the planet today. She is devoted to the rising feminine heart in the collective of humanity at this time, and believes that seeding women's circles and empowering feminine wisdom all over the world is the most effective path to support this mission. She has been leading women's circles since she was sixteen years old, and is now an author and speaker who has been mentoring, teaching, and coaching women and girls to find their authentic voice and power for over seventeen years. She leads retreats and workshops internationally, and provides a variety of online leadership and empowerment programs for women all over the world.

She graduated Magna Cum Laude with her BA in Anthropology and Religion from Boston University, and holds her Master's degree in

Depth and Counseling Psychology from Pacifica Graduate Institute. As a trained therapist and counselor, a certified life coach, an E-RYT yoga teacher, and a Reiki Master Teacher, she integrates all of these healing and therapeutic approaches in her empowerment work with women. While at Pacifica, she dove deep into the fields of comparative mythology, feminine spirituality, therapeutic counseling, and archetypal psychology, all of which are integrated into her courses and coaching programs today.

She is the author of *Conscious Feminine Leadership for Our Time and the Power of Circle, Reclaim Your Power*, as well as the companion *Reclaim Your Power Guidebook and Creativity Journal*. She is the creator of the **Reclaim Your Power** Pathway, the Lead from Love Women's Transformational Leadership Program, and the Creatrix Mastermind Experience.

She currently lives with her husband, Jonathan, and their two children, Luna and Maui, in beautiful Encinitas, California.

How to Learn More about Laura's Work:
Laura offers a variety of women's healing, empowerment, and transformational leadership courses and coaching programs. She provides group virtual circle experiences and programs, self-study online courses, as well as a variety of live in-person events and retreats. Laura's signature program, *Reclaim Your Power*, is an expansion of the pathway and processes in this guidebook, and an opportunity for you

to connect with a community of women from all over the world on your journey of self-exploration, empowerment, and healing together.

You can learn more about Laura and all of her offerings here at: **LauraJSwan.com**

Suggested Reading and Additional Resources

Laura's Website:
Here you will find a wealth of additional programs, products, and free resources from Laura for women's healing, empowerment, and leadership:
Laurajswan.com

Find Laura on Facebook and stay regularly connected:
www.facebook.com/laurajaneswan

Follow Laura on Instagram:
@laura_j_swan

Books and Suggested Reading:

Circle of Stones: Woman's Journey to Herself
By Judith Duerk

Women Who Run with the Wolves: Myths and Stories of the Wild Woman Archetype
By Clarissa Pinkola Estes

The Destiny of Women is the Destiny of the World
By Guru Rattana, PhD

Eating in the Light of the Moon: How Women Can Transform Their Relationship with Food Through Myths, Metaphors, and Storytelling
by Anita A. Johnston PhD.

The Power of Myth (book and DVD series)
by Joseph Campbell and Bill Moyers

The Light Between Us: Stories from Heaven, Lessons for the Living
By Laura Lynne Jackson

Wheels of Life: A User's Guide to the Chakra System
by Anodea Judith

Goddesses in Every Woman: Powerful Archetypes in Women's Lives
By Jean Shinoda Bolen, MD

The Heroine's Journey: Women's Quest for Wholeness
By Maureen Murdock

Grandmother's Counsel the World: Women Elders Offer Their Vision for Our Planet
by Carol Schaefer

A Woman's Worth
By Marianne Williamson

The Law of Divine Compensation: On Work, Money, and Miracles
by Marianne Williamson

Pussy: A Reclamation
by Regena Thomashauer

The Soul of Money: Transforming Your Relationship with Money and Life
By Lynne Twist

Half the Sky: Turning Oppression into Opportunity for Women Worldwide
By Nicholas D. Kristof and Sheryl WuDunn

Urgent Message from Mother: Gather the Women, Save the World
By Jean Shinoda Bolen, MD

I Am Malala: The Girl Who Stood Up for Education and Was Shot by the Taliban
By Malala Yousafzai and Christina Lamb

When God Was a Woman: The landmark exploration of the ancient worship of the Great Goddess and the eventual suppression of women's rights.
By Merlin Stone

The Red Tent
By Anita Diamant